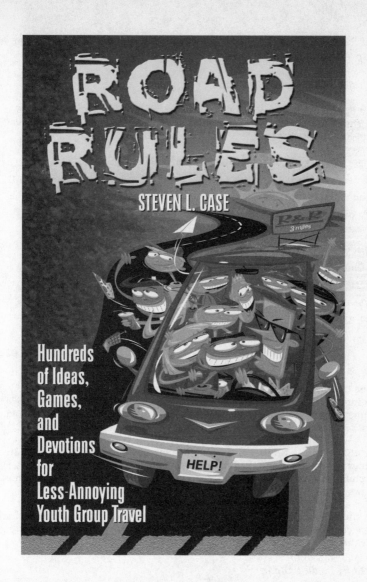

ROAD RULES

STEVEN L. CASE

Hundreds
of Ideas,
Games,
and
Devotions
for
Less-Annoying
Youth Group Travel

Youth Specialties

ZONDERVAN™

WWW.ZONDERVAN.COM

Road Rules : Hundreds of Ideas, games and Devotions for Less-Annoying Youth Group Travel

Copyright © 2003 Youth Specialties

Youth Specialties Books, 300 South Pierce Street, El Cajon, California 92020, are published by Zondervan Publishing House, 5300 Patterson Avenue Southeast, Grand Rapids, Michigan 49530

Library of Congress Cataloging-in-Publication Data

Case, Steve L., 1964-

Road rules : hundreds of ideas, games, and devotions for less-annoying

youth group travel / by Steven L. Case.

p. cm.

ISBN 0-310-25100-1 (pbk.)

1. Church group work with youth. 2. Travel--Religious

aspects--Christianity. I. Title.

BV4447.C3795 2003

259'.23--dc21

2002155886

Web site addresses listed in this book were current at the time of publication. Please contact Youth Specialties via e-mail (YS@YouthSpecialties.com) to report URLs that are no longer operational and replacement URLs if available..

Edited by Linda Bannan

Cover and interior design by Paz Design

Printed in the United States of America

03 04 05 06 07 / / 10 9 8 7 6 5 4 3 2 1

DEDICATION

This book is dedicated to Rev. Chuck Graham, who always made the journey as much fun as the destination.

ACKNOWLEDGMENTS

I would like to thank all my fellow youth workers who submitted ideas for this book whether they were used or not. May God bless your ministries and keep you safe on your journeys.

I would like to thank Dave Urbanski and all those at Youth Specialties who helped create the book in your hands.

I would like to say I'm sorry to Kristin and Megan, the sisters I once left behind at McDonald's while on a road trip.

I would like to thank the original creators of the game "punch buggy" (whomever you are) and all the other creators of classic car games who never got your due.

I would like to thank 7-Eleven and all other convenience stores and drive-thrus that sell coffee.

contents

The THEOLOGY of the ROAD

SOME OF THE GREATEST road trips ever taken are recorded in the Bible.

While technically not a road trip, Noah had one of the first and the best. Some folks can simply pack up and go, but Noah was not one of those people. The preparation for the trip itself took nearly a hundred and twenty years. His to-do list was massive. No church van existed that could haul all of the supplies God wanted Noah to carry, so he had to go out and build the biggest U-Haul the world has ever seen. Noah was a man of great patience. (A sure sign that he was a youth minister.) He was also a man of great obedience. The Bible tells us Noah did everything God commanded of him. We're not just talking about the 40 days and 40 nights. Don't forget, once it stopped

WHILE TECHNICALLY NOT A ROAD TRIP, NOAH HAD ONE OF THE FIRST AND THE BEST.

The
THEOLOGY
of the
ROAD

raining, Noah and the others were on the ark for nearly a year. Shem and Ham were in the back of the ark the whole time asking, "Are we there yet? Are we there yet?"

Moses was probably the next most famous road trip traveler. God called Moses into ministry several times before he actually decided to accept the job. Their conversation probably went something like this...

God: I want you to take my people on a road trip.

Moses: You don't want me. I'll screw it up.

God: I'll go with you.

Moses: Who do I say sent me?

God: Tell them I did.

Moses: What if they don't believe me?

At this point God did some really cool special effects that would have sent any normal youth worker but Moses running for the hills.

Moses: Cool tricks. But I have this speech impediment.

God: Take an assistant.

Moses: I don't know what to say when I get there.

God: I'll tell you what to say when the time comes.

So Moses went. He did all the things God told him to do. Along the way he encountered some discipline problems that added additional time to his journey but, all in all, you could say he accomplished what he set out to do.

(And that's the measure of a good road trip...that and keeping track of all the receipts.)

Jesus was a homebody. Most of his work was within walking distance of the town where he grew up. He did some one- and two-day trips but nothing as big or as far as Noah and Moses, but he did do some impressive things with rest stops and road food.

GOD CALLED MOSES INTO MINISTRY SEVERAL TIMES BEFORE HE ACTUALLY DECIDED TO ACCEPT THE JOB.

So why didn't our Lord and Savior go cruising from town to town in a big ol' 15-passenger van? Why didn't he have a big white one with the words JC AND THE DISCIPLES emblazoned across the side, painted in flames...okay, not flames... water maybe. Giant waves. It would have been a cool illustration for children's Bibles. So why didn't he?

The disciples would have started arguing right away... "Master, who gets to ride shotgun?"

Jesus would say, "He who wants to ride shotgun with my Father must ride in the back seat where the air conditioner is broken, and Bartholomew has smelly feet. You can not ride shotgun until you are willing to fix a flat with me."

We're only talking twelve permission slips here, and there couldn't have been all that many insurance carriers in those days.

Peter was the most impulsive of the group. He'd be the one who kept punching the radio buttons. Plus his brother, Andrew, was along. Have you ever had siblings in the same van? Jesus would have had to keep separating them. Andrew would be drawing that "invisible line" down the center.

Then there's Phillip, the guy with all the questions. Why is it that some people just can't shut up on long car trips? Between him and Thomas it's a wonder Jesus didn't just turn the van around and go home.

Matthew would be there with this little ledger. He'd have all the change counted out for every toll booth in Judea and ask, "Jesus, did you get a receipt?" He's also the guy who'd get really upset if the map wasn't folded correctly.

SO WHY DIDN'T OUR LORD AND SAVIOR GO CRUISING FROM TOWN TO TOWN IN A BIG OL' 15-PASSENGER VAN?

The
THEOLOGY
of the
ROAD

Thad and James (no, the other one) are like those two kids who never say much, and you never know they're around until you pull out of the rest stop without them.

Simon was a zealot. He questioned all authority and refused to do any of the group work. Yeah, we all want one of those on a mission trip.

Somehow you just know Judas is that guy who always had to go to the bathroom.

Jesus called James and John "the sons of thunder," which is probably not the best nickname to have when you've got thirteen people cooped up in a van. Nobody would want to sit with them!

Years later the apostle Paul was a road master. He converted to Christ while on a road trip, and he pretty much never got off the road after that. His schedule lightened up while he was in prison, but as soon as he was out, he was back on the road again.

Road trips have always been a vital part of youth ministry, though not everyone on the administrative board will agree with that. You could take thirty kids on a trip to a far-away city. You can feed the homeless. You can build a playground for homeless children. You can have wonderful worship services where teens connect with God in a very real way. You can have a homeless man have a heart attack, and one of YOUR teenagers can bring him back from the jaws of death! Then you can come home. Your students can stand up and give testimony about the trip. You can show the videos and slides to your congregation and bring them to tears with the sheer amount of love they see the kids bringing to the world.

THEN: Someone will come up to you and say, "I just wish we could help the needy in our own community."

JESUS CALLED JAMES AND JOHN "THE SONS OF THUNDER," WHICH IS PROBABLY NOT THE BEST NICKNAME TO HAVE WHEN YOU'VE GOT THIRTEEN PEOPLE COOPED UP IN A VAN.

There's always one. (Okay, there are probably several, but there's at least one who has the nerve to say something to you about it.)

These the people believe that a road trip is about the people you are serving. This is true, but there's something more. A mission trip is not just about ministering to others. It's about turning your teenagers into disciples of Jesus Christ.

If you were to try to organize your mission trip locally, you would always have one kid who just needs to miss "just one day" because of a dentist appointment. Every kid would have that sense that, "I can go home and talk to mom and dad at the end of the day."

Taking the kids on the road pulls them out of their comfort zones. It puts them in a place they may be unfamiliar with. It creates a sense of reliance on themselves and on each other. They may see things that make them uncomfortable and know that mom isn't going to pop up and tell them it's going to be okay.

Road trips can be a road to change. A lot of teens have never been away from home without mommy and daddy along. This is their first experience on their own. It's their first time seeing life's tragedies up close. It's the first time they have to deal with people who bug them and not have the option to go home at night. It's their first time to feel as if God is with them in a very real sense. When we take a road trip, we experience life outside of school, work, and home. By leaving what we know on the outside, we leave what we know on the inside at the same time. We open up to new experiences that we see and hear, as well as new experiences that we feel in our hearts and souls.

Without a doubt, most of the impact of Youth Mission trips does not happen to those being served but to the youths themselves.

A MISSION TRIP IS NOT JUST ABOUT MINISTERING TO OTHERS. IT'S ABOUT TURNING YOUR TEENAGERS INTO DISCIPLES OF JESUS CHRIST.

The THEOLOGY of the ROAD

Jesus never said, "I am the destination"; he said, "I am the way." Perhaps one of the reasons he never took a road trip is that he himself was a road trip. Jesus is "the way". The Bible is a "light unto the path." Guided tours may reduce some of the stress, but they also reduce the adventure. Following Christ should be an adventure every single day.

When Jesus proclaimed The Great Commission, he told his followers to go into ALL THE WORLD. The known world at that time was comparatively small. We didn't hear about it in America until years afterward. Jesus wasn't just saying go around the planet; he was saying we should go into new communities and cultures. The reason Jesus said, "Go" then is the same reason he tells us to "Go" now. We must go into the world and experience it. We must see, hear, and touch cultures that we didn't know existed. If we don't understand them, how can we minister to them?

WE MUST GO INTO THE WORLD AND EXPERIENCE IT. WE MUST SEE, HEAR, AND TOUCH CULTURES THAT WE DIDN'T KNOW EXISTED.

SCRIPTURES of the ROAD

(What Does the Bible Have to Say about Road Trips?)

JESUS ANSWERED, "I AM the way and the truth and the life. No one comes to the Father except through me." (John 14:6)

Jesus is a road trip! We spend a lot of time searching for Jesus. As if he is out there someplace, and we have to go and find him. The truth is, Jesus does not refer to himself as the destination. Jesus calls himself THE WAY. Jesus is not at the end of the journey. Jesus IS the journey. When we take a church road trip, either for fun or for mission, we experience Jesus. He is the way.

THE TRUTH IS, JESUS DOES NOT REFER TO HIMSELF AS THE DESTINATION. JESUS CALLS HIMSELF THE WAY.

SCRIPTURES
of the
ROAD
(What Does the
Bible Have to Say
about Road Trips?)

He said, "If I have found favor in your eyes, my lord, do not pass your servant by. Let a little water be brought, and then you may all wash your feet and rest under this tree. Let me get you something to eat, so you can be refreshed and then go on your way—now that you have come to your servant."

"Very well," they answered, "do as you say."

So Abraham hurried into the tent to Sarah. "Quick," he said, "get three seahs of fine flour and knead it and bake some bread."

Then he ran to the herd and selected a choice, tender calf and gave it to a servant, who hurried to prepare it. He then brought some curds and milk and the calf that had been prepared, and set these before them. While they ate, he stood near them under a tree. (Genesis 18:3-8)

> WHEN YOU
> TRAVEL
> TOGETHER,
> MEALS ARE A
> GREAT
> TIME TO
> BUILD
> RELATIONSHIPS.

Pop-Tarts and a bag of trail mix only go so far. You can be cheap and try to cut costs, but food probably isn't the place to do that. When you travel together, meals are a great time to build relationships. It's a time to be "not traveling," a time to be stationary and laugh and talk and share with one another. Don't skip meals in the interest of time or money. Rethink your plans and spend time talking when you are not in a van.

→→AND THEY'RE OFF! →→→→

So the man went to the house, and the camels were unloaded. Straw and fodder were brought for the camels, and water for him and his men to wash their feet. Then food was set before him, but he said, "I will not eat until I have told you what I have to say." (Genesis 24:32-33)

Don't forget why you travel in the first place. Throughout the Scriptures we see that God is the starting point of many journeys. When God starts something rolling, it is best to follow through. Understand at the same time that if God started it rolling, then it will finish the way he wants it to. So don't be discouraged by roadblocks you meet along the way.

→→PORT-A-CHURCH

Then Moses said to the Israelites, "See, the Lord has chosen Bezalel son of Uri, the son of Hur, of the tribe of Judah, and he has filled him with the Spirit of God, with skill, ability and knowledge in all kinds of crafts—to make artistic designs for work in gold, silver and bronze, to cut and set stones, to work in wood and to engage in all kinds of artistic craftsmanship. And he has given both him and Oholiab son of Ahisamach, of the tribe of Dan, the ability to teach others. He has filled them with skill to do all kinds of work as crafts- men, designers, embroiderers in blue, purple and scarlet yarn and fine linen, and weavers—all of them master craftsmen and designers. So Bezalel, Oholiab, and every skilled person to whom the Lord has given skill and ability to know how to carry out all the work of constructing the sanctuary are to do the work just as the Lord has commanded." (Exodus 35:30-36:1)

You don't need a sanctuary to worship. You don't even need to pull over to one of those

YOU DON'T NEED A SANCTUARY TO WORSHIP. YOU DON'T EVEN NEED TO PULL OVER TO ONE OF THOSE PICTURESQUE KODAK-MOMENT SPOTS.

SCRIPTURES
of the
ROAD
(What Does the
Bible Have to Say
about Road Trips?)

picturesque Kodak-Moment spots. You can have a worship service anyplace. Remember why you are on this trip. When you plan the schedule add in 15 minutes at a rest stop to pray and thank God for all you've been given. Bezalel was an artist, and God filled him with inspiration to create a portable church in the wilderness. You can do the same. Find a picnic table. Build an altar. Have a communion service right out there in the open. Let everyone bring something into the mix. You are all in this together.

➜➜BEEN THERE. DONE THAT. BOUGHT THE T-SHIRT➜➜➜

> But Moses said, "Please do not leave us. You know where we should camp in the desert, and you can be our eyes. If you come with us, we will share with you whatever good things the Lord gives us."
> (Numbers 10:31-32)

Whenever possible take along someone who has been there. This applies both literally and figuratively. If you head out on a journey, take someone who has been where you are going. Call people who live at your destination and get advice from them as well.

Remember, your students look to you as someone who has been there. You've already been through what they're going through. You have the experience. You may not be at your own destination yet, but you can reach out and bring along someone who is lagging behind.

➜➜WHY ARE WE DOING THIS AGAIN?➜➜➜

> And our elders and all those living in our country said to us, "Take provisions for your journey; go and meet them and say to them, 'We are your servants; make a treaty with

FIND A
PICNIC
TABLE. BUILD
AN ALTAR.
HAVE A
COMMUNION
SERVICE
RIGHT OUT
THERE IN THE
OPEN.

us.' This bread of ours was warm when we packed it at home on the day we left to come to you. But now see how dry and moldy it is. And these wineskins that we filled were new, but see how cracked they are. And our clothes and sandals are worn out by the very long journey."
(Joshua 9:11-13)

Remember that some Road Trips are not for a vacation. Often we have to give something up and do without. This is not necessarily a bad thing. Getting away from the tons of material things we store up and getting down to basics can clear our heads. Even if your trip is for fun, remember that everything you do is for God's own glory. Mission trips are expected to be difficult and tiring. From this kind of adversity we can come together. In other words: Whatever doesn't kill you makes you stronger.

⇢⇢EAT HERE. GET GAS. ⇢⇢⇢⇢

We have both straw and fodder for our donkeys and bread and wine for ourselves your servants—me, your maidservant, and the young man with us. We don't need anything."

"You are welcome at my house," the old man said. "Let me supply whatever you need. Only don't spend the night in the square."
(Judges 19:19-20)

Most of us no longer travel by donkey, but it doesn't hurt to take care of the church van while you travel. Be ready. Take what you need, but if hospitality is offered to you, take it! Don't get so caught up in the idea of roughing it or

GETTING AWAY FROM THE TONS OF MATERIAL THINGS WE STORE UP AND GETTING DOWN TO BASICS CAN CLEAR OUR HEADS.

doing without that you turn down an opportunity to refuel yourself both physically (a good night's rest) and emotionally (quiet time and prayer).

SCRIPTURES
of the
ROAD
(What Does the Bible Have to Say about Road Trips?)

FRIENDSHIPS CREATED ON ROAD TRIPS ARE OFTEN THE STRONGEST OF ALL.

⇢⇢BUDDY SYSTEM⇢⇢⇢⇢

When she heard in Moab that the Lord had come to the aid of his people by providing food for them, Naomi and her daughters-in-law prepared to return home from there. With her two daughters-in-law she left the place where she had been living and set out on the road that would take them back to the land of Judah.

Then Naomi said to her two daughters-in-law, "Go back, each of you, to your mother's home. May the Lord show kindness to you, as you have shown to your dead and to me. May the Lord grant that each of you will find rest in the home of another husband."

Then she kissed them and they wept aloud and said to her, "We will go back with you to your people."

But Naomi said, "Return home, my daughters. Why would you come with me? Am I going to have any more sons, who could become your husbands? Return home, my daughters; I am too old to have another husband. Even if I thought there was still hope for me—even if I had a husband tonight and then gave birth to sons—would you wait until they grew up? Would you remain unmarried for them? No, my daughters. It is more bitter for me than for you, because the Lord's hand has gone out against me!"

*At this they wept again. Then Orpah kissed
her mother-in-law good-by, but Ruth clung
to her.*

*"Look," said Naomi, "your sister-in-law is
going back to her people and her gods. Go
back with her."*

*But Ruth replied, "Don't urge me to leave
you or to turn back from you. Where you go
I will go, and where you stay I will stay.
Your people will be my people and your
God my God. Where you die I will die, and
there I will be buried. May the Lord deal
with me, be it ever so severely, if anything
but death separates you and me." When
Naomi realized that Ruth was determined
to go with her, she stopped urging her.
(Ruth 1:6-18)*

Friendships created on road trips are often the
strongest of all. The adversity and difficulties can
bring people together and cement them there.
When we don't have anyone else to rely on, we
turn to each other.

Naomi tells Ruth to make it easier on herself
and go back to her family. Ruth chooses to stay,
and the two of them begin a road trip that will
end years down the road. Out of this friendship
will come a child. The child will eventually lead us
to David. From the house of David we will get a
carpenter who will change the world. Road trips
do not end when the van pulls back into the
church parking lot. Relationships born on the
road will continue long after the individuals arrive
back home.

→→STOP BY OUR GIFT SHOP→→→→

*"By all means, go," the king of Aram
replied. "I will send a letter to the king of
Israel." So Naaman left, taking with him*

SCRIPTURES
of the
ROAD
(What Does the Bible Have to Say about Road Trips?)

ten talents of silver, six thousand shekels of gold, and ten sets of clothing. (2 Kings 5:5)

Arriving at Jerusalem with a very great caravan—with camels carrying spices, large quantities of gold, and precious stones—she came to Solomon and talked with him about all that she had on her mind. (1 Kings 10:2)

Never go anywhere empty-handed. Take gifts for those who show you hospitality. Even if the gift is a song from your choir or a thank you note that everyone signed. You can travel a lot of ways. The way you travel will affect the way others are received. The way others travel will affect the way you are received. Take care of those who put you up, feed you, and give you rest.

→→ROAD TESTED→→→→

...but no stranger had to spend the night in the street, for my door was always open to the traveler. (Job 31:32)

While this verse is a kind thought, it comes from Job's long speech where he unloads his list to God. Job talks about the ways he feels put upon and used.

God responds with a list of his own, basically saying did you make the universe? Did you make the earth? Put the oceans in place? Sculpt a mountain? Job, of course, has done none of these, and he says so. When the road gets tough and we start to feel the Why-Mes setting in, remember that God is in charge of the trip. All things will work out the way they are supposed to. Stop looking at the hard part, and look for the lesson.

→→GOD RIDES SHOTGUN→→→→

A miktam of David.
Keep me safe, O God,
for in you I take refuge.

TAKE

CARE OF

THOSE WHO PUT

YOU UP,

FEED YOU,

AND GIVE

YOU REST.

I said to the Lord, "You are my Lord;
apart from you I have no good thing."
As for the saints who are in the land,
they are the glorious ones in whom is all
my delight.
The sorrows of those will increase
who run after other gods.
I will not pour out their libations of blood
or take up their names on my lips.

Lord, you have assigned me my portion and
my cup;
you have made my lot secure.
The boundary lines have fallen for me in
pleasant places;
surely I have a delightful inheritance.

I will praise the Lord, who counsels me;
even at night my heart instructs me.
I have set the Lord always before me.
Because he is at my right hand,
I will not be shaken.

Therefore my heart is glad and my
tongue rejoices;
my body also will rest secure,
because you will not abandon me to
the grave,
nor will you let your Holy One
see decay.
You have made known to me
the path of life;
you will fill me with joy in
your presence,
with eternal pleasures at
your right hand.
(Psalm 16:1-11)

> GOD DOES NOT GIVE DIRECTIONS AND THEN LET US GO OFF ON OUR OWN.

God never stands and points. We should never think of God as that old guy at the gas station who

SCRIPTURES
of the
ROAD
(What Does the
Bible Have to Say
about Road Trips?)

comes over to the car and gives us confusing directions. God gets in the car with us. He joins us on the journey. He sits there and keeps us company and tells us where to turn and then makes the turn with us. God does not give directions and then let us go off on our own. God is right with us at every turn.

→→WHEN THE ROAD GETS ROCKY→→→→

A song of ascents.

I lift up my eyes to the hills—
where does my help come from?
My help comes from the Lord,
the Maker of heaven and earth.

He will not let your foot slip—
he who watches over you will not slumber;
indeed, he who watches over Israel
will neither slumber nor sleep.

The Lord watches over you—
the Lord is your shade at your right hand;
the sun will not harm you by day,
or the moon by night.

The Lord will keep you from all harm—
he will watch over your life;
the Lord will watch over your coming
and going
both now and forevermore. (Psalm 121:1-8)

IF YOU GET LOST, IT'S NOT HIS FAULT, BUT LOOK FOR THE LESSON AS YOU WANDER.

God will watch over your journey. This does not mean that you can be stupid. Don't go places you shouldn't go. Don't do things that could cause you or your fellow travelers harm. But remember that God will watch over and protect you. If you get lost, it's not his fault, but look for the lesson as you wander. Sometimes God talks to us in surprising ways. If you feel lost, turn back to God. God is watching and won't let you wander very far.

WE'RE IN THIS TOGETHER

Let your eyes look straight ahead,
fix your gaze directly before you.
Make level paths for your feet
and take only ways that are firm.
Do not swerve to the right or the left;
keep your foot from evil. (Proverbs 4:25-27)

Be one-minded in your trip—whether it is for a mission or just for fun. Remind your group that it is everybody's job to make the trip run smoothly—not just a few. Everyone shares the work and the preparation. Wandering off or letting someone else do your share of the work will cause bumps in the road. If everyone works together the path will be level and smooth.

DON'T GET LOST

The highway of the upright avoids evil;
he who guards his way guards his life.
(Proverbs 16:17)

Being away from home can present a whole new batch of distractions. You and your crew may run up against problems that you would never encounter at home. On the road we have to work harder than ever to be the servants God has called us to be.

MOVIN' RIGHT ALONG

There will be a highway for the remnant of
his people
that is left from Assyria,
as there was for Israel
when they came up from Egypt. (Isaiah
11:16)

Isaiah speaks about when all of the people gather for the Messiah's arrival. God creates a highway that will bring us all together. Road trips

ON THE ROAD WE HAVE TO WORK HARDER THAN EVER TO BE THE SERVANTS GOD HAS CALLED US TO BE.

SCRIPTURES
of the
ROAD
(What Does the
Bible Have to Say
about Road Trips?)

are great bonding experiences. Be sure you take time out from the busy schedule to worship and pray with the whole group. God will use the trip as a highway to bring your group together in his name.

→→CAN WE GO HOME YET?→→→→

> Then I heard the voice of the Lord saying, "Whom shall I send? And who will go for us?"
>
> And I said, "Here am I. Send me!"
> (Isaiah 6:8)

God says, "Whom shall I send?" And the youth worker in the back of the room raises his hand and says, "I'll go." Later after he has spent his seventh hour behind the wheel of a van and is ready to turn around and smack the kid behind him who keeps making "that noise," he wonders why did God send me?

We volunteer for road trips. God asked. We volunteered. We said, "Yeah, I'll work with teens." It's a decision that can be difficult, but in the long run is not one that we regret. We serve a loving God. God does not let his servants down. Ever.

WE SERVE
A LOVING
GOD.
GOD DOES
NOT LET HIS
SERVANTS
DOWN.

→→PACK LIGHT→→→→

> "Therefore, son of man, pack your belongings for exile and in the daytime, as they watch, set out and go from where you are to another place. Perhaps they will understand, though they are a rebellious house. During the daytime, while they watch, bring out your belongings packed for exile. Then in the evening, while they are watching, go out like those who go into exile.
> (Ezekiel 12:3-4)

Preparation is everything. Some people know how to pack a suitcase; others just throw their stuff into the bag. God wanted his followers to know that even the packing of their belongings had meaning to those who saw them travel. Wherever you go on your trip remember that there are those who watch you because you are followers of God.

HIDING IS FUTILE

> The word of the Lord came to Jonah son of Amittai: "Go to the great city of Nineveh and preach against it, because its wickedness has come up before me."
>
> But Jonah ran away from the Lord and headed for Tarshish. He went down to Joppa, where he found a ship bound for that port. After paying the fare, he went aboard and sailed for Tarshish to flee from the Lord.
>
> Then the Lord sent a great wind on the sea, and such a violent storm arose that the ship threatened to break up. All the sailors were afraid and each cried out to his own god. And they threw the cargo into the sea to lighten the ship.
>
> But Jonah had gone below deck, where he lay down and fell into a deep sleep. The captain went to him and said, "How can you sleep? Get up and call on your god! Maybe he will take notice of us, and we will not perish."
>
> Then the sailors said to each other, "Come, let us cast lots to find out who is responsible for this calamity." They cast lots and the lot fell on Jonah.

WHEREVER YOU GO ON YOUR TRIP REMEMBER THAT THERE ARE THOSE WHO WATCH YOU BECAUSE YOU ARE FOLLOWERS OF GOD.

SCRIPTURES
of the
ROAD
(What Does the Bible Have to Say about Road Trips?)

"BUT THE LORD PROVIDED A GREAT FISH TO SWALLOW JONAH, AND JONAH WAS INSIDE THE FISH THREE DAYS AND THREE NIGHTS."

So they asked him, "Tell us, who is responsible for making all this trouble for us? What do you do? Where do you come from? What is your country? From what people are you?"

He answered, "I am a Hebrew and I worship the Lord, the God of heaven, who made the sea and the land."

This terrified them and they asked, "What have you done?" (They knew he was running away from the Lord, because he had already told them so.)

The sea was getting rougher and rougher. So they asked him, "What should we do to you to make the sea calm down for us?"

"Pick me up and throw me into the sea," he replied, "and it will become calm. I know that it is my fault that this great storm has come upon you."

Instead, the men did their best to row back to land. But they could not, for the sea grew even wilder than before. Then they cried to the Lord, "O Lord, please do not let us die for taking this man's life. Do not hold us accountable for killing an innocent man, for you, O Lord, have done as you pleased." Then they took Jonah and threw him overboard, and the raging sea grew calm. At this the men greatly feared the Lord, and they offered a sacrifice to the Lord and made vows to him.

But the Lord provided a great fish to swallow Jonah, and Jonah was inside the fish three days and three nights.

From inside the fish Jonah prayed to the Lord his God. He said:

"In my distress I called to the Lord,
and he answered me.
From the depths of the grave I called for help,
and you listened to my cry.
You hurled me into the deep,
into the very heart of the seas,
and the currents swirled about me;
all your waves and breakers
swept over me.

I said, 'I have been banished
from your sight;
yet I will look again
toward your holy temple.'
The engulfing waters threatened me,
the deep surrounded me;
seaweed was wrapped around my head.
To the roots of the mountains I sank down;
the earth beneath barred me in forever.
But you brought my life up from the pit,
O Lord my God.

"When my life was ebbing away,
I remembered you, Lord,
and my prayer rose to you,
to your holy temple.

"Those who cling to worthless idols
forfeit the grace that could be theirs.
But I, with a song of thanksgiving,
will sacrifice to you.
What I have vowed I will make good.
Salvation comes from the Lord."

And the Lord commanded the fish, and it vomited Jonah onto dry land.
(Jonah 1:1-2:10)

"WHEN MY LIFE WAS EBBING AWAY, I REMEMBERED YOU, LORD, AND MY PRAYER ROSE TO YOU, TO YOUR HOLY TEMPLE."

SCRIPTURES
of the
ROAD
(What Does the
Bible Have to Say
about Road Trips?)

The very first thing that God says to Jonah... the very first word out of God's mouth is, "Go." God tells a lot of people to go. Moses tried to talk his way out of the job. Jonah simply runs the other direction. Moses is the guy who said, "You don't want me, God." Then he stood there and made his case.

Jonah headed for the hills. Picture it in your imagination like a Road Runner cartoon. The coyote just realizes he's about to get hit with something heavy, and he turns to run. Jonah does that. He tried to hide. (Hint: You can't hide from God.) Jonah winds up in all sorts of trouble on his trip because he didn't just follow God's plan from the get-go.

He winds up in the belly of the fish. Then he decides to pray. Figures. How many times do we go cruising along, and then when the tire blows or when we find out our map was written in 1973, we start praying? "Okay, God. You're in charge. I'm listening this time. I'll do what you want." So many of our road trip troubles are our own creation. If we just stop and listen before we even get in the church van, we'll do better.

"HONEY,
I'LL BE GONE
FOR A
FEW YEARS,
BUT DON'T
WORRY.
NO, REALLY, I
DON'T
NEED A
MAP."

→→MEN NEVER ASK
FOR DIRECTIONS→→→→

> After Jesus was born in Bethlehem in Judea,
> during the time of King Herod, Magi from
> the east came to Jerusalem and asked,
> "Where is the one who has been born king
> of the Jews? We saw his star in the east
> and have come to worship him."
> (Matthew 2:1-23)

Now that was a trip! Most of us gripe because we have a long drive to church. These guys made a journey of thousands of miles to see Jesus. Why? They may have studied ancient text that said the

Messiah was coming and a star would be the sign. Maybe God spoke to them and told them to go. Who knows?

Imagine trying to explain that to the Mrs. Wisemen. "Honey, I'll be gone a few years, but don't worry. No, really, I don't need a map. We're going to follow a star. Yes, a star." Imagine the faith involved in just beginning, let alone continuing, the journey.

> When King Herod heard this he was disturbed, and all Jerusalem with him. When he had called together all the people's chief priests and teachers of the law, he asked them where the Christ was to be born. "In Bethlehem in Judea," they replied, "for this is what the prophet has written:
>
> " 'But you, Bethlehem, in the land of Judah, are by no means least among the rulers of Judah;
> for out of you will come a ruler who will be the shepherd of my people Israel.'"
>
> Then Herod called the Magi secretly and found out from them the exact time the star had appeared. He sent them to Bethlehem and said, "Go and make a careful search for the child. As soon as you find him, report to me, so that I too may go and worship him."

Ever get lost and have someone give you bad directions? Herod had other things in mind. This probably looked like the beginning of the end for him. His own wise men, the chief priests, knew the Scriptures well enough to tell him that his time was nearly over.

So Herod put his plan into motion. Send them on their way, get them to tell me where the baby

EVER GET LOST AND HAVE SOMEONE GIVE YOU BAD DIRECTIONS? HEROD HAD OTHER THINGS IN MIND.

SCRIPTURES
of the
ROAD
(What Does the
Bible Have to Say
about Road Trips?)

is, then I can end this. But if he put any stock in his priests at all, he knew he couldn't end it. He knew his days were numbered. He probably never had a decent night's sleep the rest of his life.

After they had heard the king, they went on their way, and the star they had seen in the east went ahead of them until it stopped over the place where the child was. When they saw the star, they were overjoyed. On coming to the house, they saw the child with his mother Mary, and they bowed down and worshiped him. Then they opened their treasures and presented him with gifts of gold and of incense and of myrrh.

We usually see the wise men show up at the stable. More than likely, Jesus was about two years old when they found him. They brought gifts. However, they didn't stop at the Bethlehem Toys-R-Us on the way. We're told they brought gold, frankincense, and myrrh. The gold probably helped finance Joseph's upcoming road trip to Egypt. (See the importance of preplanning!) Frankincense was something you gave to a king, and myrrh was something you put on a dead body. This was probably the equivalent to bringing a coffin to a baby shower.

THEY BROUGHT
GIFTS.
HOWEVER, THEY
DIDN'T
STOP AT THE
BETHLEHEM
TOYS-R-US
ON THE WAY.

And having been warned in a dream not to go back to Herod, they returned to their country by another route.

See you have to be flexible. The wise men spent all that time getting there, and then they found out they had to go home a different direction. If you get rigid in your travel plans, you'll get into trouble. God may have another plan. Open yourself up to see where he wants you to go.

When they had gone, an angel of the Lord appeared to Joseph in a dream. "Get up," he said, "take the child and his mother and escape to Egypt. Stay there until I tell you,

*for Herod is going to search for the child to
kill him."*

*So he got up, took the child and his mother
during the night and left for Egypt, where
he stayed until the death of Herod.*

One good trip deserves another. Joseph gets a
pot of gold right when he's got to pack up everything and move. Ever plan a trip on a shoestring
budget? God made the trip easier. Joseph probably
had a nice little business going by this time, and
he packed up and left. God doesn't always give us
a choice. We see that in the Bible a lot of times.
God says, "Go," and we go.

→→THE GREATEST TRAVELING COMPANION→ → → →

*Now that same day two of them were going
to a village called Emmaus, about seven
miles from Jerusalem. They were talking
with each other about everything that had
happened. As they talked and discussed
these things with each other, Jesus himself
came up and walked along with them; but
they were kept from recognizing him.*

*He asked them, "What are you discussing
together as you walk along?"*

*They stood still, their faces downcast. [18]
One of them, named Cleopas, asked him,
"Are you only a visitor to Jerusalem and do
not know the things that have happened
there in these days?"*

"What things?" he asked.

*"About Jesus of Nazareth," they replied. "He
was a prophet, powerful in word and deed
before God and all the people. The chief
priests and our rulers handed him over to*

"AS THEY **TALKED** AND **DISCUSSED** THESE **THINGS** WITH EACH OTHER, **JESUS** HIMSELF CAME UP AND **WALKED ALONG** WITH THEM; BUT **THEY** WERE KEPT FROM RECOGNIZING **HIM.**"

SCRIPTURES
of the
ROAD
(What Does the
Bible Have to Say
about Road Trips?)

be sentenced to death, and they crucified him; but we had hoped that he was the one who was going to redeem Israel. And what is more, it is the third day since all this took place. In addition, some of our women amazed us. They went to the tomb early this morning but didn't find his body. They came and told us that they had seen a vision of angels, who said he was alive. Then some of our companions went to the tomb and found it just as the women had said, but him they did not see."

He said to them, "How foolish you are, and how slow of heart to believe all that the prophets have spoken! Did not the Christ have to suffer these things and then enter his glory?" (Luke 24:13–26)

Jesus met his disciples on the road. They were on their way to some place, and they were talking about all that had happened. Jesus met them, traveled with them, and talked to them. Jesus will do the same for us. He's there when it's quiet and there's nothing else to talk about. He's there when we see students begin to connect with each other. He's there when we get so tired that we can't keep going, but we somehow manage to do so anyway. Jesus is with us on the road.

JESUS
IS WITH US
ON THE
ROAD.

⇥⇥THANK GOD, WE'RE HERE! ⇥⇥⇥⇥

But when our time was up, we left and continued on our way. All the disciples and their wives and children accompanied us out of the city, and there on the beach we knelt to pray. (Acts 21:5)

Paul knew the value of prayer. Not just for those being prayed for but for those doing the praying. Sometimes journeys are dangerous. Paul's faith made him stronger. It gave strength to those who came to see him off and to those who traveled with him. Pray as a group before you leave on your trip. Pray each day before you head out. Pray each night. And pray when you return home.

→→YOU THOUGHT YOUR TRIP WAS ROUGH →→

When a gentle south wind began to blow, they thought they had obtained what they wanted; so they weighed anchor and sailed along the shore of Crete. Before very long, a wind of hurricane force, called the "northeaster," swept down from the island. The ship was caught by the storm and could not head into the wind; so we gave way to it and were driven along. As we passed to the lee of a small island called Cauda, we were hardly able to make the lifeboat secure. When the men had hoisted it aboard, they passed ropes under the ship itself to hold it together. Fearing that they would run aground on the sandbars of Syrtis, they lowered the sea anchor and let the ship be driven along. We took such a violent battering from the storm that the next day they began to throw the cargo overboard. On the third day, they threw the ship's tackle overboard with their own hands. When neither sun nor stars appeared for many days and the storm continued raging, we finally gave up all hope of being saved.

After the men had gone a long time without food, Paul stood up before them and said: "Men, you should have taken my advice not to sail from Crete; then you would have

"BUT NOW I URGE YOU TO KEEP UP YOUR COURAGE, BECAUSE NOT ONE OF YOU WILL BE LOST; ONLY THE SHIP WILL BE DESTROYED."

SCRIPTURES
of the
ROAD
(What Does the Bible Have to Say about Road Trips?)

"SO KEEP UP YOUR COURAGE, MEN, FOR I HAVE FAITH IN GOD THAT IT WILL HAPPEN JUST AS HE TOLD ME."

spared yourselves this damage and loss. But now I urge you to keep up your courage, because not one of you will be lost; only the ship will be destroyed. Last night an angel of the God whose I am and whom I serve stood beside me and said, 'Do not be afraid, Paul. You must stand trial before Caesar; and God has graciously given you the lives of all who sail with you.' So keep up your courage, men, for I have faith in God that it will happen just as he told me. Nevertheless, we must run aground on some island."

On the fourteenth night we were still being driven across the Adriatic Sea, when about midnight the sailors sensed they were approaching land. They took soundings and found that the water was a hundred and twenty feet deep. A short time later they took soundings again and found it was ninety feet deep. Fearing that we would be dashed against the rocks, they dropped four anchors from the stern and prayed for daylight. In an attempt to escape from the ship, the sailors let the lifeboat down into the sea, pretending they were going to lower some anchors from the bow. Then Paul said to the centurion and the soldiers, "Unless these men stay with the ship, you cannot be saved." So the soldiers cut the ropes that held the lifeboat and let it fall away.

Just before dawn Paul urged them all to eat. "For the last fourteen days," he said, "you have been in constant suspense and have gone without food—you haven't eaten anything. Now I urge you to take some food. You need it to survive. Not one of you will lose a single hair from his head." After he said this, he took some bread and gave thanks to God in front of them all. Then he broke it and began to eat. They were all encouraged and ate some food themselves. Altogether there were 276 of us on board. When they had eaten as much as they wanted, they lightened the ship by throwing the grain into the sea.

When daylight came, they did not recognize the land, but they saw a bay with a sandy beach, where they decided to run the ship aground if they could. Cutting loose the anchors, they left them in the sea and at the same time untied the ropes that held the rudders. Then they hoisted the foresail to the wind and made for the beach. But the ship struck a sandbar and ran aground. The bow stuck fast and would not move, and the stern was broken to pieces by the pounding of the surf.

The soldiers planned to kill the prisoners to prevent any of them from swimming away and escaping. But the centurion wanted to spare Paul's life and kept them from carrying out their plan. He ordered those who could swim to jump overboard first and get to land. The rest were to get there on planks or on pieces of the ship. In this way everyone reached land in safety.

Once safely on shore, we found out that the island was called Malta. The islanders showed us unusual kindness. They built a fire and welcomed us all because it was raining and cold. Paul gathered a pile of brushwood and, as he put it on the fire, a

"THE ISLANDERS SHOWED US UNUSUAL KINDNESS. THEY BUILT A FIRE AND WELCOMED US ALL BECAUSE IT WAS RAINING AND COLD."

SCRIPTURES
of the
ROAD
(What Does the
Bible Have to Say
about Road Trips?)

viper, driven out by the heat, fastened itself on his hand. When the islanders saw the snake hanging from his hand, they said to each other, "This man must be a murderer; for though he escaped from the sea, Justice has not allowed him to live." But Paul shook the snake off into the fire and suffered no ill effects. The people expected him to swell up or suddenly fall dead, but after waiting a long time and seeing nothing unusual happen to him, they changed their minds and said he was a god.

*There was an estate nearby that belonged to Publius, the chief official of the island. He welcomed us to his home and for three days entertained us hospitably. His father was sick in bed, suffering from fever and dysentery. Paul went in to see him and, after prayer, placed his hands on him and healed him. When this had happened, the rest of the sick on the island came and were cured. They honored us in many ways and when we were ready to sail, they furnished us with the supplies we needed.
(Acts 27:13-28:10)*

SOMETIMES
WHEN WE'RE
ON THE ROAD,
IT SEEMS
AS IF
EVERYTHING
GOES
WRONG.

Talk about your Road Trip from hell! Sometimes when we're on the road, it seems as if everything goes wrong. Not just one thing, but one thing on top of the other. It's as if each bad break we get causes six more, and no matter where we turn it's all going to fall apart.

Every trip leader in the world has felt this way at some point. If we all had the faith of Paul, these little problems on the road wouldn't bother us. But we don't, and they do. Paul constantly had to reassure his fellow travelers that everything would be okay, and in fact everything did turn out to be okay.

God sent us. God is with us. God will not leave us to our own devices, or we would wind up wrecking everything. You may not see the light in the darkness right away. You may not even see it until the trip is long over, but those problems you face will make you stronger, and in the long run they are worth the effort.

➟➟ STARTING, STOPPING, AND RESTING ➟➟

> On the fourth day they got up early and he prepared to leave, but the girl's father said to his son-in-law, "Refresh yourself with something to eat; then you can go."
> (Judges 19:5)

> Jacob's well was there, and Jesus, tired as he was from the journey, sat down by the well. It was about the sixth hour. (John 4:6)

> He had the camels kneel down near the well outside the town; it was toward evening, the time the women go out to draw water.
> (Genesis 24:11)

Start in the morning; rest at noon; stop in the evening. As the great philosopher Ferris Bueller once said, "Life moves pretty fast. If you don't stop and look around, you're gonna miss it."

Yes, it's a road trip, but that doesn't mean you have to spend all your time on the road. Plan when you'll travel, but also plan when you'll stop. Get out of the van. Take a break. Know when to start, stop, and take a break.

➟➟ BIBLICAL REST STOPS ➟➟➟➟

> He instructed the one in the lead: "When my brother Esau meets you and asks, 'To whom do you belong, and where are you going, and who owns all these animals in front of

YES, IT'S A ROAD TRIP, BUT THAT DOESN'T MEAN YOU HAVE TO SPEND ALL YOUR TIME ON THE ROAD.

SCRIPTURES
of the
ROAD
(What Does the
Bible Have to Say
about Road Trips?)

you?' then you are to say, 'They belong to your servant Jacob. They are a gift sent to my lord Esau, and he is coming behind us.'"

He also instructed the second, the third and all the others who followed the herds: "You are to say the same thing to Esau when you meet him. And be sure to say, 'Your servant Jacob is coming behind us.' " For he thought, "I will pacify him with these gifts I am sending on ahead; later, when I see him, perhaps he will receive me." So Jacob's gifts went on ahead of him, but he himself spent the night in the camp.
(Genesis 32:17–21)

Jacob chilled out before he went to meet his brother. This was the brother that he cheated out of the family inheritance years before. The Jacob who returned home was not the same as the one who left. He stopped to rest, and he sent his people on ahead of him. He had to prepare himself to meet his brother again. Jacob wound up wrestling with an angel. The angel dislocated Jacob's hipbone. Years ago people believed the hip was the center of pride in the body. The angel dislocated Jacob's pride so he could repair his relationship with his brother.

THE ANGEL DISLOCATED JACOB'S PRIDE SO HE COULD REPAIR HIS RELATIONSHIP WITH HIS BROTHER.

We all need to take rest stops in life and prepare ourselves for what's next. Sometimes we have to wrestle with something and leave it behind before we can move ahead.

→→BE QUIET, AND TRUST→→→→

Then Moses led Israel from the Red Sea and they went into the Desert of Shur. For three days they traveled in the desert without finding water. When they came to Marah, they could not drink its water because it was bitter. (That is why the place is called

*Marah.) So the people grumbled against
Moses, saying, "What are we to drink?"*

*Then Moses cried out to the Lord, and the
Lord showed him a piece of wood. He
threw it into the water, and the water
became sweet.*

*There the Lord made a decree and a law for
them, and there he tested them. He said, "If
you listen carefully to the voice of the Lord
your God and do what is right in his eyes,
if you pay attention to his commands and
keep all his decrees, I will not bring on
you any of the diseases I brought on
the Egyptians, for I am the Lord, who
heals you."*

*Then they came to Elim, where there were
twelve springs and seventy palm trees, and
they camped there near the water.
(Exodus 15:22-27)*

You think you have to deal with backseat
whiners? Moses had thousands of them. They
were generations of whiners who always complained. Moses finally cried out to God, and God
gave the people a rest stop. God used this opportunity to say, "Shut up. Trust me. Everything is going
to be okay." And it was.

That's good advice for all of us. It's good
advice to throw into the back seat when
you've heard, "Are we there yet?" for the one-
thousandth time.

→→TAKE TIME FOR OTHERS→→→→

*Now he had to go through Samaria. So he
came to a town in Samaria called Sychar,
near the plot of ground Jacob had given to
his son Joseph. Jacob's well was there, and*

YOU THINK
YOU HAVE TO
DEAL WITH
BACKSEAT
WHINERS?
MOSES HAD
THOUSANDS OF
THEM.

SCRIPTURES
of the
ROAD
(What Does the Bible Have to Say about Road Trips?)

EVEN AFTER A LONG DAY ON THE ROAD WHEN HE FINALLY STOPPED AND PUT HIS FEET UP FOR A MOMENT, HE STILL REACHES OUT TO THOSE WHO ARE OUTCASTS.

Jesus, tired as he was from the journey, sat down by the well. It was about the sixth hour.

When a Samaritan woman came to draw water, Jesus said to her, "Will you give me a drink?" His disciples had gone into the town to buy food.)

The Samaritan woman said to him, "You are a Jew and I am a Samaritan woman. How can you ask me for a drink?" (For Jews do not associate with Samaritans.)

Jesus answered her, "If you knew the gift of God and who it is that asks you for a drink, you would have asked him and he would have given you living water."

"Sir," the woman said, "you have nothing to draw with and the well is deep. Where can you get this living water? Are you greater than our father Jacob, who gave us the well and drank from it himself, as did also his sons and his flocks and herds?"

Jesus answered, "Everyone who drinks this water will be thirsty again, but whoever drinks the water I give him will never thirst. Indeed, the water I give him will become in him a spring of water welling up to eternal life." (John 4:4-14)

Jesus never wasted an opportunity. Even after a long day on the road when he finally stopped and put his feet up for a moment, he still reaches out to those who are outcasts. He never stops being Jesus even though that must have been exhausting. Few people would talk to the woman at the well, and none would believe. Jesus spoke to her. Jesus forgave her. Jesus offered her what he offers us all. Living water. Life itself. Who are we to say "No"?

CHAPTER

ROAD PRAYERS

BEFORE YOU PILE IN.

God, we are so full of anticipation that
we can hardly stand ourselves. We
have enough energy in the circle to
power a small city. Help us focus that
energy, God. Help us create an atmosphere where we can grow and shine
and experience your light. Then, help
us reflect that light to others. We are
at the beginning, God. All that we
hope for is just ahead of us. Go with
us, God. Lift us when we are tired.
Guide us when we are lost. Join us
when we call on your spirit. Go with
us, God. Amen.

HELP US
CREATE AN
ATMOSPHERE
WHERE WE CAN
GROW AND
SHINE AND
EXPERIENCE
YOUR
LIGHT.

ROAD PRAYERS

→→A PRAYER TO BEGIN A MISSION TRIP→→→→

God, bring our minds and hearts into a pure focus. We are your servants. Help us to remember that above all things. We are your servants. Let us be your hands. Let us be your eyes. Let us be your ears. We are your children. We are here to take care of each other. Sometimes the world is a scary place, God. We wonder how it can get so bad. Help us to understand that your children must care for each other, and in doing so, bring your presence into the world. Amen.

→→A PRAYER TO BEGIN A FUN TRIP→→→→

God, we stand before you now wanting to get on the road. We can't wait, God. We can't wait for the laughter. We can't wait for the fun. Help us take this one moment and understand that the laughter and the fun and the friendships and the joy are all gifts from you. Help us to show appreciation. Help us to remember who to thank. We look to you to get us through the bad times. Now help us look to you to be with us when we laugh. Amen.

→→A PRAYER FOR WHEN YOU'RE BROKEN DOWN BY THE SIDE OF THE ROAD→→→→

God, we know that you do not cause bad things to happen. We know that you take all things, both good and bad, and make them work together. Give us patience, God. Give us strength. Open our eyes to the big picture so that we can see things we might have missed. Show us the lesson. Let us learn it well, and send us back on our way. Amen.

HELP US TAKE THIS ONE MOMENT AND UNDERSTAND THAT THE LAUGHTER AND THE FUN AND THE FRIENDSHIPS AND THE JOY ARE ALL GIFTS FROM YOU.

➜➜ A PRAYER FOR WHEN YOU ARE LOST

God, we need more than a map right now. Send down the flashing neon sign that points us in the right direction. We are not lost, God. We are in your presence wherever we go. How can we be lost? Calm our anxieties. Place your reassuring hand on our shoulders. Show us the way, but don't let us miss a moment of the experience. Let us take it all in, God. Show us the way. Amen.

➜➜ A PRAYER FOR WHEN EVERYONE IS ON EDGE ➜

God, there are times when we walk a fine line. When we compact molecules into a small space, they will eventually explode. Cut us the slack that we have trouble showing to others. Grant patience when we feel impatient. Help us to think before we speak. The Bible says that you cannot tame a tongue, but help us to hold it in check, God. Let us lift each other up instead of cutting each other down. Let us hold each other close instead of pushing each other away. Grant us space. Grant us respect. Grant us love. Amen.

➜➜ A PRAYER FOR MIDWEEK ➜➜➜➜

God, our time is half over. It seems as if it just started, and at the same time it seems as if we've been at it forever. Let us look at all we've done and smile. Help us to not lose focus on what we have yet to do. Give us strength, God. Show us that it's not over. Show us that we are not done yet. Renew our energy so that we may finish the journey as we began it. Renew our minds so that that we don't lose focus on what is ahead of us. Amen.

SIDEBAR ON THE GO

GRANT us PATIENCE WHEN WE FEEL IMPATIENT. HELP US to THINK BEFORE WE SPEAK.

THE WAY

ROAD PRAYERS

→→ A PRAYER FOR PATIENCE →→→→

The days are long, God. Give us just a little bit of your love so that the next time we think we can't take any more, we can. Give us the ability to deal with those we don't think we can deal with. Give us the courage to get through the situations that seem intolerable. These moments of frustration and aggravation are nothing compared to the good that we are doing. Open our eyes to the possibilities. Do not let us close them to the world. Don't let us shut down. We are your children, and we need your love right now. Amen.

→→ A PRAYER FOR REST →→→→

God, the body grows weary. Give us peace. Give us a quiet night. It's hard to keep the soul energetic when the body is so tired. Keep us healthy, God. Calm the things that are running around in our brains, and give us peace. Relax our tension. Renew us physically, mentally, emotionally, and spiritually. Fill us up with your love so that we may continue to do all the things you have asked us to do. Don't let us tire out. Renew us. Amen.

→→ A PRAYER FOR UNDERSTANDING →→→→

God, focus our brains in the right directions. Help us to open ourselves so that we are more concerned with understanding others than with being understood ourselves. Give us ears that listen beyond the words. Give us eyes that see beneath the surface. Help us to understand each other so that we may grow closer to one another. Open the lines of communication so we do not feel as if we are talking to a wall. Give us just a small sense of the understanding you give to us, and we will be fine. Amen.

➦➦A PRAYER FOR GUIDANCE

God, there are a lot of ways to get lost. We can point to a spot on the map and know exactly where we are and yet still feel as if we are wandering in a dark cave with no flashlight. Call out to us, God. Let us follow your voice. Stand beside us and point. Show us YOUR map. Help us to go where you want us to go, so that we can become what you want us to become. Amen.

➦➦A PRAYER FOR THE NIGHT BEFORE THE LAST DAY

God, we have experienced so much. It's as if our brains and souls are on overload. Tomorrow when we rise, we will go home. We will leave behind all that we have done, and soon it will exist in our memories. Help us to look forward to the new life that awaits us because we are not the same people, God. Help us reflect the changes in ourselves to those back home. Let the new day be a new day for the rest of our lives. Amen.

➦➦A PRAYER FOR THE LAST DAY➦➦➦➦

God, it doesn't seem as if we started out just _____ days ago. On the other hand it seems as if we've been at this for a very long time. We are tired and weary, God. We've accomplished much. We've grown closer to each other, and in doing so we have grown closer to your Son. As we leave this place, may we leave behind a small bit of that light that drew us to you. May it brighten the path and lead others to you as well. Amen.

➦➦A PRAYER OF THANKS TO CLOSE THE JOURNEY➦➦➦➦

God, it's over. We're home. Thank you for getting us home again. Thank you for bringing us here safely. Thank you for the blessings you have

> THANK YOU FOR THE BLESSINGS YOU HAVE GIVEN TO US, EVEN IF THEY DON'T SEEM LIKE BLESSINGS JUST YET.

given to us, even if they don't seem like blessings just yet. We are your tired servants, God. Thank you for these wonderful people and the ways that you have shown us your presence these past _____ days. Amen.

→→A PRAYER FOR WHEN THINGS GET TENSE→→→→

God, we can learn from your creation. When molecules are packed into a small space they bounce off of each other until something eventually explodes. Help us keep our patience, God. Help our fuses be long. And keep our noses in joint and keep our undies unbunched. We are your children, God. Help us treat each other that way. Amen.

→→A BLESSING ON THE PLACE WHERE YOU WORKED→→→→

May God continue to bless this place. May God's angels surround and protect you. May you be able to build upon the work done and create a forest from this tree that was planted here. Amen.

→→A BLESSING FOR THE HOME YOU STAYED IN→→→→

May God bless your house. May you open the doors to angels unaware. Let all who pass through your doors feel the warmth and love that you have shown to us. Amen.

→→A BLESSING FOR THE WAITER OR WAITRESS WHO SERVED YOU→→→→

May the tips be generous. May your smile come easily. May God give strength to your feet, and energy to your body, and uplift your spirit. Amen.

MAY YOU BE ABLE TO BUILD UPON THE WORK DONE AND CREATE A FOREST FROM THIS TREE THAT WAS PLANTED HERE.

48

AVOIDING the SLEEP-DEPRIVED NASTIES

OKAY, PICTURE THIS AND see if it doesn't strike you as just a little familiar. You are sitting at table in one of the finer fast food establishments. You have a super whatever burger in front of you. It is your third this week. Across from you is a young man who is sucking his milkshake through a plastic straw. He is nearing the bottom, and when he gets there, he is going to make "the sound" again. You've sat near him for four different meals, and every time he gets to the bottom of the cup he sucks on the straw as if maybe if he sucks on the straw hard enough to make a vein pop out on his pointy little head he might

ACROSS FROM YOU IS A YOUNG MAN WHO IS SUCKING HIS MILKSHAKE THROUGH A PLASTIC STRAW... HE IS GOING TO MAKE "THE SOUND" AGAIN.

AVOIDING the SLEEP- DEPRIVED NASTIES

just find some hidden trove of chocolate that would have otherwise been ignored.

Sssssssssssssssssssssskkkkkkkkkkkkrrrrrrrrrrp

Sssssssssssssssssssssssskkkkkkkkkkkkrrrrrrrrp

Sssssssssssssssssssssssssskkkkkkkkkkkrrrrrrrp

And you, the youth minister, summon all your energy and somehow manage to stop yourself from reaching across the table, grabbing him by the front of his T-shirt, and in one smooth motion batting the cup from his hand.

SLURP!

milkshake

You, my youth ministering friend, have a case of the Sleep-Deprived Nasties. That little known, but very real, medical condition that takes otherwise happy funny youth ministers and turns them into touchy coiled springs that will go "Spronnnnnnnnng!" if someone just looks at them the wrong way.

For centuries youth ministers have suffered from this common and dangerous malady. The Sleep-Deprived Nasties (SDN) can strike anyone regardless of gender, age, or experience in youth ministry. SDN is a common occurrence on road trips, mission trips, and lock-ins. The severity of SDN depends on the individual to a certain extent, but it can turn even the sweetest, levelheaded volunteer into someone who shouldn't be allowed near the cutlery.

YOUTH SUFFERING FROM SDN OFTEN TAKE IT OUT ON EACH OTHER.

Youth suffering from SDN often take it out on each other. On the fourth day of the choir tour, students start keeping track of who is and who isn't pulling their own weight in the work area. Ironically, they only keep track of those who work less than THEY do. SDN in teens often can bond them together but for the wrong reasons. Teens with SDN will gang up on one unsuspecting member who can suddenly go from having a good time to having a horrible one.

Occasionally SDN results in feelings of anger or resentment toward those being served on a mission trip. I once took a group to Appalachia. We spent several days "winterizing" a man's home. He spent the week watching us. Under the SDN influence the teens began to grow angry. "It's his home. He's not even helping. He's just sitting there watching us do it for him."

So what can you do? What are some ways that you, as the youth leader, can avoid the effects of SDN and create a safer, more enjoyable environment for the youth and youth leaders in your group? Here are some easy tips to help things go smoother.

→→YES, IT'S YOU→→→→

Understanding that you have the problem is half the battle. We all put up with the occasional jab or ribbing from our teenagers. We're adults, remember? But the Sleep Deprived Nasties can cause us to take these verbal barbs way too personally. Educate your students to SDN before you leave. If you feel you have a case of SDN, inform the group immediately. It is better that they know early and can use their own restraint before you are likely to put them in one. If a kid is throwing verbal darts your way, take him aside and let him know that you have SDN and would appreciate him keeping it to himself.

I own one of the greatest youth ministry tools ever invented. It's the X-treme Gulp cup from 7-Eleven—a red insulated mug that holds a whopping 52 ounces of your favorite caffeinated beverage. My students all know this mug. They've seen it. I even passed it around the circle once. I'm not a morning person. I tell them all from the beginning, "If you don't see me with my cup in the morning, don't talk to me. You can come up and

IF YOU FEEL YOU HAVE A CASE OF SDN, INFORM THE GROUP IMMEDIATELY. IT IS BETTER THAT THEY KNOW EARLY AND CAN USE THEIR OWN RESTRAINT BEFORE YOU ARE LIKELY TO PUT THEM IN ONE.

AVOIDING the SLEEP-DEPRIVED NASTIES

give me a hug but NO QUESTIONS. Once I have the cup in my hand, give me a few minutes, and then come talk to me." Forewarned is forearmed. It is that sort of blatant honesty that allows me to return home with the same number of students I had when I left.

⇢⇢LIGHTS OUT! COME ON... I REALLY MEAN IT THIS TIME!⇢⇢⇢⇢

If you are on a mission trip or a choir tour or even a ski trip, you owe it to those around you to be at your best. Let your teens know that these trips are not vacations. If you are not able to give one hundred percent of yourself, then you are cheating those you came to help as well as those around you who are giving all they've got.

Set a reasonable lights-out time, and stick to it. Be the hard-nosed youth director. If you set 10:30 as the lights-out time, then set 10:00 as the head-for-bed time. Otherwise you'll have students who decide to go brush their teeth at 10:29. If the group does not make the lights-out time the first night, adjust the time on the earlier side. Aim for 9:45 as the get-ready time. Lights out means just that. Everyone is horizontal and prepared to sleep. You can offer an evening devotion at this time and a final prayer.

CREATE **ONE HOUR** EVERY AFTERNOON WHERE **EVERYONE MUST** BE HORIZONTAL.

⇢⇢POWER NAP⇢⇢⇢⇢

Take a nap! You'd be amazed how much easier things can be after a short snooze. If you don't want to call it nap time, try something more like H-Hour. Many business books use the term "power-nap." Create one hour every afternoon where everyone must be horizontal. They don't have to sleep, but they must be horizontal and quiet. Read a book. Listen to music. Whatever. Just get horizontal. Do not allow adult leaders (yourself included) to use this time as a mini-planning meeting. Again, rest is vital.

THE GOOD, THE BAD, AND THE UGLY

Some people can leap right out of bed in the mornings. They can smile as they greet the new day and glow back at the sunshine. Others tend to hit mornings head on and are lucky to walk away from the collision.

Here's an example. Once there was a college girl named Debbie. Debbie was a night person, and her roommate was a morning person. The first week of school Debbie's roommate dragged her out of bed at 6:00 a.m. on a Saturday morning. She pointed out the window and said, "Look, Debbie, a rainbow. That's God's way of saying 'Good Morning, Debbie!'" Debbie then punched her. They weren't roommates after that. (True story.)

What will get you through the week is simple common courtesy. If you are a night person and you cannot sleep, be courteous to those around you, and lie quietly. If you are morning person determined to get up an hour before the youth leaders' alarm to watch the sunrise or go jogging, keep it down as you get ready and let the door close quietly.

"I'll sleep in the van." or "I'll sleep at home." are not options. Nothing is louder than someone trying to talk quietly in the middle of the night. Often a church floor (usually cold tile but sometimes a stiff carpet) does little to foster a good night's sleep. If you know you'll be sleeping on a church floor, do yourself a favor and buy an air mattress. Encourage your students to do the same. Splurge. Get the nice one and an electric air pump. It will mean the difference between four hours of sleep and five hours of sleep—which makes it one of the best investments of your career.

IF YOU ARE A **NIGHT PERSON** AND YOU **CANNOT SLEEP**, BE COURTEOUS TO **THOSE AROUND YOU**, AND LIE **QUIETLY.**

AVOIDING the SLEEP-DEPRIVED NASTIES

`0.6`

SCREAM SESSION

One incredibly effective way to fight the SDN is to allow your youth leaders time to themselves. If an errand needs to be run or the van needs gas, send two youth leaders out together and just let them scream. Encourage it. Let them roll down the windows and shout. Tell them to scream wildly inappropriate things about the teenager who is most vexing them. (Yes, I'm aware of how bad that sounds, but it is incredibly therapeutic.) Give them space, and they will come back to you as new people.

Don't forget to schedule yourself some time too. You are in charge, after all. You can't be on twenty-four hours a day. Give yourself a break, and let it all out. (Be sure you are far enough away—say, 10 to 20 miles.)

→→IN GOD WE TRUST...
FOR TEENAGERS THERE'S
DUCT TAPE→→→→

IF AN ERRAND NEEDS TO BE RUN OR THE VAN NEEDS GAS, SEND TWO YOUTH LEADERS OUT TOGETHER AND JUST LET THEM SCREAM.

Make sure your group knows exactly how things are before you even leave home. Explain that the trip is a matter of trust. You have to be able to trust them enough so you can close your eyes at night and not worry about who might be sneaking out. If you find yourself up late because you heard that someone went for a walk the night before, then that trust factor has been violated and you can take the appropriate action. It's an old trick but a small piece of tape on the outside of a door will let you know if anyone goes out walking in the night.

→→DEBRIEF DOES NOT MEAN
TO PANTS SOMEBODY→→→→

Not all SDN is caused by physical exhaustion. In many cases your youth are having brand new experiences. They are seeing new things and meeting new people. These things can be mentally and emotionally exhausting. Be sure to have a debriefing time each day to allow individuals time to process information.

THERE'S ALWAYS HELP

If SDN seems to creep into your group, plan evening devotions that revolve around verses such as "How can you get the speck out of your neighbor's eye when you have a log in your own?" or "Love does not keep a record of wrongs." These great passages can go a long way while sitting in a darkened room around a candle.

Jesus talked about agape. Agape is that special kind of love that requires nothing in return. When SDN begins to make us judgmental about those we are traveling with or those we are serving, we need to remember that Jesus loved everyone. He even loved the ones who put him on the cross.

Then again, he never had to listen to that milkshake noise.

...REMEMBER THAT JESUS LOVED EVERYONE... THEN AGAIN, HE NEVER HAD TO LISTEN TO THAT MILKSHAKE NOISE.

CC and IIAYDFWI

TWO RULES THAT WILL GET

you through the trip.

A long time ago the Pharisees tried to trip Jesus up. They wanted to discredit him. These were guys who spent their lives following every letter of the law. These were guys who argued for a living. So when they came up to Jesus and said, "What is the greatest commandment?" they were hoping to goad him into an argument. They were hoping he would choose from Moses' top-ten list, and then they would have nine more to throw at him. It was a nifty trick but it didn't work.

A LONG TIME AGO THE PHARISEES TRIED TO TRIP JESUS UP. THEY WANTED TO DISCREDIT HIM.

**CC
and
IIAYDFWI**

They asked Jesus, "What is the greatest commandment?" He said, "I'll give you two. Love God with all your heart and all your mind and all your soul. AND love your neighbor as yourself."

Great answer. All other commandments could come under these two. The Pharisees had nothing to argue with him about.

Like Jesus' reply to the Pharisees, these are two rules for most road trips that all other rules can come under. By all means list out every rule you expect the teens to abide by, but get them to memorize these two.

CC

IIAYDFWI

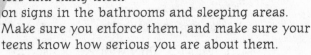

List these, as is, everywhere you can. Print them on letters and hang them on signs in the bathrooms and sleeping areas. Make sure you enforce them, and make sure your teens know how serious you are about them.

Here's what they mean.

→→CC→→→→

CC is common courtesy. A little of this from everybody, and your week will go smoothly.

If you made the mess...clean it up.

If you used it...put it back.

If you broke it...fix it or tell the adult leader.

If you dirtied the dish...wash it.

If you wore it...put it your laundry bag.

If your feet smell like a road kill that's been buried under a chicken coop for six years...use some foot powder.

CC IS **COMMON COURTESY.** A **LITTLE** OF THIS FROM **EVERYBODY,** AND YOUR WEEK WILL **GO** **SMOOTHLY.**

If you are going to do THAT...go to another room.

And for God's sake...flush.

If someone makes a dumb mistake...help them. Your turn may be next.

See? Common Courtesy. It's not that hard. Really. It's not.

⇢⇢IIAYDFWI⇢⇢⇢⇢

This one is harder to remember because it has more letters. Ready? If it ain't yours...don't fool with it. (IIAYDFWI)

It's sort of like common courtesy only more specific. Stay out of other people's stuff.

If someone leaves the booth to get a napkin, stay out of her fries. If there is a CD lying on the table and it isn't yours, don't take it. If you suddenly get the idea that it would be funny to get someone's underwear and run it up the flagpole, don't.

This rule can also apply to certain wanted or unwanted displays of affection. Romance can blossom on road trips, and as a youth worker, you will need all the help you can get.

⇢⇢ONE MORE⇢⇢⇢⇢

This third rule can be added in to the list. Ready? There is no such thing as a PRACTICAL joke.

Too often practical jokes can create hurt feelings and leave scars. Targets of practical jokes are just that...targets. Those most susceptible to practical jokes are often the ones who would be most hurt by them. Practical jokes can quickly turn into joke wars—us against them.

Lay out your opinions for your youth. Tell them the basics: Clothes are not to be run up flagpoles. You shouldn't have shaving cream unless your

> IT'S SORT OF LIKE COMMON COURTESY ONLY MORE SPECIFIC. STAY OUT OF OTHER PEOPLE'S STUFF.

beard is out of control. Squirt guns are great for hot summer days, but they have no place in the van. Snipes don't exist. A picture of your butt is not funny. Putting something in someone else's food can make them choke.

Everyone can remember a time when they were pointed at, ridiculed, or made fun of. There is no such thing as a practical joke.

THERE IS

NO SUCH

THING

AS A

PRACTICAL

JOKE.

CHAPTER

Is That a BUZZ SAW in Your HEAD or Are You Just LISTENING to MUSIC?

A WORD ABOUT MUSIC

and personal music systems.

Policies regarding personal music systems vary from denomination to denomination. Actually, they vary from church to church within the denomination. Okay, the whole music thing is pretty much up to the person running the show at the time. I've seen churches that have no music policy whatsoever and don't care what CDs come along. Others say you can only bring Christian Rock. Some have taken the "What Would Jesus Listen To?" approach. Some churches simply avoid

> OKAY, THE WHOLE MUSIC THING IS PRETTY MUCH UP TO THE PERSON RUNNING THE SHOW AT THE TIME.

Is That a BUZZ SAW in Your HEAD or Are You Just LISTENING to MUSIC?

the problem by banning personal CD players all together.

Try this idea as you plan your next road trip. It will save you hours of aggravation in the long run.

You can bring this idea up at the informational meeting before the trip, or you can lead it as a lesson with the teens a few months before you leave.

Ask questions like the following ones.

Is there some piece of music you listen to when you're depressed?

Is there some piece of music or band that you listen to when you want to be cheered up?

Guys: Is there some piece of music you listen to when you're on a date?

IN A SITUATION WHERE THE RIGHT ATTITUDE IS VITAL TO ACCOMPLISHING THAT GOAL, WHAT MUSIC CHOICES ARE BEST FOR THE SITUATION?

Is there a particular station you listen to when you're out driving with friends on a Saturday night with the windows rolled down?

More than likely you'll get a "Yes" reply to each of these questions? Ask them about their favorite songs or stations, and then ask them, "Why? Why do you listen to that song or that station in that situation?" Bring the group to the general consensus that music can affect your behavior.

Define the goal of the road trip. Ask the group what they want to accomplish on the road trip. In a situation where the right attitude is vital to accomplishing that goal, what music choices are best for the situation?

Then step back, and let them make the choice. Educate them. Inform them. And then trust them. Don't go policing their backpacks. Don't put out a list of banned artists.

Come to some sort of agreement like, "Yes, you can listen to that band, but if I hear one of those words come out of your mouth, then I'm taking the disc."

Make a rule that if their personal CD player sounds like a tiny belt sander on their head, then perhaps it's too loud. Personal music systems should be personal. It's not a shared experience.

And for the record—the driver always chooses the tunes!

PERSONAL MUSIC SYSTEMS SHOULD BE PERSONAL. IT's NOT A SHARED EXPERIENCE.

If ___(YOUR NAME HERE)___ AIN'T HAPPY, Then Ain't NOBODY HAPPY

HELPFUL HINTS TO HELP

you keep your sanity.

Guess what? Road trips can make you crazy. But you already knew that! The problem comes when you or one of your adult leaders is ready to explode, and you still have three more days before you head home. What then? These tips will help you reclaim your sanity, or at least help you hang on to it a little longer.

Punt. The best-laid plans of mice and men quite often go awry. Okay, let us rephrase for the youth minister, shall we? Whatever can go wrong, will go wrong. If you don't have a back-up plan for your back-up plan, you could

THESE **TIPS** WILL HELP YOU **RECLAIM** YOUR **SANITY** OR AT LEAST **HELP** YOU **HANG ON** TO IT A LITTLE LONGER.

WE ALL

WANT OUR

TEENAGERS

TO HAVE THOSE

MOUNTAINTOP

EXPERIENCES

THAT

CHANGE

THEIR LIVES,

BUT YOU

CAN'T

MAKE

THOSE HAPPEN

NO MATTER

HOW MUCH

YOU WANT

THEM TO.

wind up being stuck someplace you don't want to be. When all else fails, be ready to punt. Go with the flow. Take the situation at hand, come up with the best solution for the moment, and go with it. You have to be able to handle yourself in a crisis because difficulties will happen.

Don't push. You cannot "will" God moments to happen. We all want our teenagers to have those mountaintop experiences that change their lives, but you can't make those happen no matter how much you want them to. Much of what your teens experience on a road trip won't have an effect until months after they return. Road trips plant a seed. You can't sit over a freshly planted seed and "will" it to grow. The same applies with how an experience affects your teenagers.

Be flexible. You may have the schedule written out, but you have to be willing and able to change the plans. If the workday takes longer than expected, then switch the plans so that you can finish. If you get stuck in traffic for an hour, and it throws off everything else you were going to do that evening, you have to change plans.

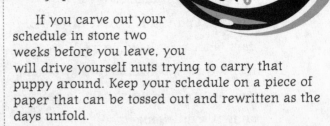

If you carve out your schedule in stone two weeks before you leave, you will drive yourself nuts trying to carry that puppy around. Keep your schedule on a piece of paper that can be tossed out and rewritten as the days unfold.

Time alone. All of the participants have to do a tremendous amount of mental processing during a road trip or mission week. Some of your students may have never experienced anything like this. In science class you learned what happens when you compress too many molecules into a small space.

They start bouncing off each other and the walls until something explodes. So schedule a few hours in a morning or afternoon to allow teens to process. Even if they all stay in the same building, they need a chance to be alone. Say, "See you at four o'clock," and let them go. (Of course for safety reasons they should never wander alone far from the place where you are staying).

Time together. It is also important to give your teens time to process without you in the room. After so many new experiences your group will start debriefing on their own. Sometimes you must put aside your own ego and let the group members fly unattended. They may have ideas and thoughts they would share with each other that they aren't ready to share with their youth minister just yet. They also may need time to talk about you, the one in charge. Give them that space. Respect their privacy. Don't eavesdrop from around the corner. If you do, it's guaranteed you'll hear something you wish you hadn't.

Don't be afraid. We love our students. We wouldn't be good youth ministers if we didn't. We love them as if they were our own children. We want to shelter them from all that is nasty and ugly. But the world is not always pretty, and some things are painful to see. As youth workers we sometimes have to put our students into places they may have never gone on their own. That's part of the job. We cannot be afraid to let our students see things that will upset them.

Have fun. If you're on a mission trip, don't forget to have a day when students can experience the opposite of work. It has been said that Albert Einstein would stop work on the bomb every day at 3:15 to watch *Beanie and Cecil,* a television cartoon show hosted by two hand puppets. Einstein believed it was vital to his work to be able to walk away from it and think with an entirely different part of the brain. Taking a day to go to an amusement park while on a mission trip is not a reward, it is a way to lift the spirit

TAKING A DAY TO GO TO AN AMUSEMENT PARK WHILE ON A MISSION TRIP IS NOT A REWARD, IT IS A WAY TO LIFT THE SPIRIT AND RENEW THE SOUL.

If (YOUR NAME HERE) AIN'T HAPPY, Then Ain't NOBODY HAPPY

GOD WILL MEET THEM IN THE TOUCH OF AN OLD PERSON'S HAND, THE SONG SUNG AROUND A FIRE, THE UNPLANNED CONVERSATIONS THAT TAKE PLACE LATE IN THE NIGHT.

and renew the soul. It is necessary for the group's continued mental health.

You are not in charge. This is perhaps the hardest lesson of all. I've noticed over the years that the more confident I get in my own leadership of such trips, the more our trips tend to unravel, and we begin to fly by the seat of our pants. It's easy to get so caught up in the logistics of being where we're supposed to be at the time we're supposed to be there that we fail to put things in God's hands. You may put together the schedule, budget the money, and drive the van, but God is in charge. If God wants you to learn, you will learn. If God wants you to see something, you will see it.

The small. Elijah stood on the mountain and looked for God in the giant fire, the earthquake, and the tornado. But God was not in any of these things. God was in the still small voice that blew across his cheek like a breeze. As youth workers, we want our students to have massive life changing experiences, but more than likely God will speak to them in that still small voice. God will meet them in the touch of an old person's hand, the song sung around a fire, the unplanned conversations that take place late in the night.

CHAPTER eight

SHOTGUN

EVERYBODY WANTS TO RIDE

in the favorite seat. Here are a few Road Rules for the coveted chair as well as a list of responsibilities that go along with it. Copy the Responsibilities List on card stock so that any student sitting in the shotgun seat can read and agree to the rules before you set off.

IF THE **ADULTS** SHOULD CHOOSE TO **GIVE UP** THAT **SEAT**, THEN IT IS **OPEN** FOR "**CALLING.**"

→→THE RULES→→→→

Who gets it first? The Shotgun seat goes to any adult leader who wants it. They have first priority. No arguments. If the adults should choose to give up that seat, then it is open for "calling."

Calling for the shotgun seat. Students may not reserve the seat in advance. One cannot "call" it for the trip home as you are loading for the beginning of the trip. Shotgun "calling" may only be done immediately prior to loading when the vehicle is in sight, and the calling must be done in the earshot of the youth leader or driver.

It's the driver's call. The driver has the right to approve or remove someone in the shotgun seat. Just as with the wing seat on an airplane, if you are not up to the responsibility, you can be moved to another seat.

Take turns. Once you have ridden in the shotgun seat, give someone else a chance.

Power of the shotgun. Sitting in the shotgun seat offers a student no more power over other students than he or she had previously. In fact, it increases the responsibility.

JUST AS WITH THE **WING SEAT** ON AN **AIRPLANE,** IF YOU ARE **NOT UP TO** THE RESPONSIBILITY, YOU CAN BE **MOVED** TO ANOTHER **SEAT.**

→→RESPONSIBILITIES LIST FOR THE SHOTGUN SEAT→→→→

(Must be read and agreed to prior to driving away.)

- *You are there to assist the driver. You will do everything you can to make the driver's job easier. This may include adding cream to coffee, picking the pickles off a burger, or helping to find a radio station.*

- *You are the driver's extra set of ears. You are the one to relay messages to the back seats and repeat messages from the back to the driver.*

- You are the driver's extra eyes. If the driver is looking for a specific street sign, then so are you.

- The shotgun seat does not mean nap time. If you travel at night or after a long day, it's your job to help keep the driver awake. Offer coffee or conversation or whatever will keep the driver focused.

- You are also in charge of tollbooth money and maps. Have the change ready to hand to the driver at the tollbooth. Keep an eye on the map. Prior knowledge of map reading and folding is a plus in your position.

- Riding shotgun may exclude you from playing certain road games if you need to assist the driver. OR you may have to lead road games or act as an official referee in certain instances.

- You are there to make the driver's job easier. (Yes, you already read that but it is worth repeating.)

YOU ARE

THERE

TO MAKE THE

DRIVER'S

JOB

EASIER.

Van ETIQUETTE or (YOUR NAME HERE) 's TOP-TEN LIST of VAN RULES

INCLUDE THIS LIST WITH

your permission slip. Have the kids sign it and turn it in with all of the other forms.

1. Do not block the driver's view with signs, undergarments, feet, or any other body part. Safety is the first concern; fun comes second.

2. The person sitting in the driver's seat has the final say-so on the selection and volume level of all music played on the vehicle's radio, tape, or CD player. You may want to share your gangsta-rap-punk-polka, but that doesn't mean the driver wants to hear it.

3. If you brought it into the van, take it out. When unloading the vehicle, do not throw aside others' belongings to get to yours. Everyone helps.

YOU MAY WANT TO SHARE YOUR GANGSTA-RAP-PUNK-POLKA, BUT THAT DOESN'T MEAN THE DRIVER WANTS TO HEAR IT.

Van ETIQUETTE
or (YOUR NAME HERE)'s
TOP-TEN LIST
of VAN RULES

4. If you made the mess, YOU clean it up. Do I look like your mother?

5. If you do not have to "go" at the scheduled rest stop, give it the old college try anyway. Making the rest of the group wait while you have your own "quiet time" is rather rude.

THE JOKE OF "WANNA HEAR THE MOST ANNOYING SOUND IN THE WORLD" IS OLD AND TIRED, AND IT LOSES ITS HUMOR AFTER THE FIRST TELLING.

6. If you can't say something nice, don't say anything at all.

7. Safety. Safety. Safety. Use common sense when playing road games.

8. Driving advice from the back seat is not always necessary or welcome.

9. The joke of "Wanna hear the most annoying sound in the world," is old and tired, and it loses its humor after the first telling.

10. Do not participate in a belching contest unless the youth leader starts it.

CHAPTER ten

ROAD HINTS

THIS LIST OF IDEAS AND thoughts comes from youth workers around the country.

IF YOU GO TO MEXICO ON A MISSION TRIP, YOU CAN NOW APPLY FOR AND SECURE VEHICLE REGISTRATION ONLINE...

→→MEXICO MISSION TRIP TIP→→→→

If you go to Mexico on a mission trip, you can now apply for and secure vehicle registration online at www.banjercito.com.mx. If you drive into the interior of Mexico past the federal checkpoint, you'll wait forever in the line at the DMV office if you don't get insurance online.

Tim and Tasha Levert

→→KID FINDER→→→→

Whenever we go to a multichurch function, concert, rally, ballgame, or amusement park, I take a Polaroid picture of each youth from head to foot. I clip these to their permission and release forms. If, God forbid, something should happen or they get lost, not only do I have a recent picture, but I have one that shows the clothes they wore that day. I am always extra careful when I am responsible for other people's kids.

Dorothy Porcher-Holland

→→CLIPBOARD QUIET→→→→

The simplest activity I ever planned for the kids to do in the van ended up being the best. I provided a clipboard with paper and pens for each kid. They spent hours writing notes, drawing pictures, and playing word games. I'd always had paper and markers, but the clipboards made the difference. It was the quietest trip we ever took. Needless to say I was astonished!

Dorothy Porcher-Holland

→→OUR LAPTOP→→→→

We had a large square piece of plywood with the edges sanded down that just fit across our laps to form a table for four. The "laptop" came along on every trip we took so we could play Phase 10, Uno, Yahtzee, et cetera. The best part was that the kids covered both sides of the board with graffiti, including dates, names, and memories. Each time we left for the latest road trip, we had reminders of our other trips and what God had done during them.

Melissa Morrow

THE BEST PART WAS THAT THE KIDS COVERED BOTH SIDES OF THE BOARD WITH GRAFFITI, INCLUDING DATES, NAMES, AND MEMORIES.

➜➜JOBS

When we go on a trip, our teens sign up for different jobs—someone to fill the gas, someone to wash windows, someone to empty the trash, someone to navigate, someone to check the oil, and some to act as luggage crew. Students do any job that needs to be done, if possible. On short trips everyone just keeps the same job, but on longer trips, we rotate. The goal is for everyone to have a job—even if it means doubling up on some. Of course if you have more than one van, you need to double up on some jobs anyway so that all vehicles are covered.

Nick Hatch

➜➜DIFFERENT PERSPECTIVES➜➜➜➜

Here's a great idea that works especially well for smaller groups, although any size group can use it. Before your next trip buy your students each a disposable camera, write their names on them, and hand them out to students. Discount warehouse stores like Sam's Club or BJ's Wholesale Club sell boxes of these cameras fairly cheap. After you return collect the cameras and have the film developed. Post the pictures with the photographer's name where everyone can see them. Kids will love seeing the different perspectives of their friends, and you'll have a ready-made scrapbook.

Tripp Walton

➜➜1-800-ENCOURAGE➜➜➜

We've all seen those signs on the trucks that ask, "How is my driving?" Well, pick up the old cell phone (especially if it is on a weekend and the rates are cheap), give the number a call, and report that it looks like the driver is doing a really good job. You might want to do a play-by-play to the dispatcher, or even compare this driving with one of the other trucks on the road ("Be grateful

THE GOAL IS FOR EVERYONE TO HAVE A JOB – EVEN IF IT MEANS DOUBLING UP ON SOME.

that you don't have that slouch from XYZ transport driving."). See if you can get the driver a raise or ask the person on the phone to call him right then and pass on the good words. The leader should always be the only one to speak.

Joe Harsel

→→FRIEND IN THE LUGGAGE RACK→→→→

Have your students stitch together a life-size, life-like mannequin out of student-donated clothes and foam. Use old nylons for skin, and add a wig, a hat, and a pair of garden gloves to finish off the giant doll. Make sure the doll is built for abuse. (Attach everything with lots of hot glue, and sew with strong fishing line) Now strap your foam kid to the top of your vehicle, and roll tape or snap photos of other folk's reactions to it as you drive along.

Keith A Turner

→→HUBCAP→→→→

When we go on a road trip with our youth group, we have everyone watch for a hubcap alongside the road. When someone spots one, we pull over (where it is safe of course), the leader (and I stress leader only) gets out, gets the hubcap, and each person on the trip signs it. After we return, we place it on our wall called Power Net Road Warriors (Power Net is our group's name). The hubcaps become lasting monuments to our trips.

Jay Crouch

→→HOOD ORNAMENT→→→→

Before we leave on each trip, we tie put a different grill or hood ornament to the front of the van. A few things we have tied on are a pink flamingo, a big old coffee can that people can put

BEFORE
WE LEAVE ON
EACH TRIP,
WE TIE A
DIFFERENT
GRILL
OR HOOD
ORNAMENT
TO THE FRONT
OF THE VAN.

stuff in or donate change, and a wooden-handled glass scrubber. It's fun to see some of the looks we get when we drive down the road. At the end of church camp, we took off the flamingo, passed it around for every person at camp to sign, then strapped it back on, took it home, and hung in our youth room.

Billy Fly

→→STATE LINE→→→→

When we're on a road trip, we stop to take a picture at the state sign of our destination. Most states in the United States have a sign that welcomes interstate travelers to the state. So we stop the vans, get everybody out, and take a group picture. We have pictures from Alabama, South Dakota, Virginia, Florida, Tennessee, and this summer we will add Michigan. Most of my youth cringe when they know we're getting close to the state line of our destination. But it's fun to stop on the side of an interstate and take a picture. Most people probably think we're crazy!

R.W. Moody, Jr.

→→VAN THEMES→→→→

If our youth group takes a trip by van, we assign a theme to each van and then decorate. This is a blast. The leaders keep the themes a surprise until the trip. We find cheap decorations, or we make them ourselves. Some of the themes we've used include Power Rangers, jungle, hippie, and Pocahontas. Let your imagination lead you.

Allyson Clark

MOST STATES IN THE UNITED STATES HAVE A SIGN THAT WELCOMES INTERSTATE TRAVELERS TO THE STATE. SO, WE STOP THE VANS, GET EVERYBODY OUT, AND TAKE A GROUP PICTURE.

→→VOICE OF ENCOURAGEMENT→→→→

Prior to the trip get several parents together and have them record funny or serious messages—maybe even morning devotions on a CD or tape. As you travel each day, play these words of encouragement for your students. We went on a mission trip and each day as we traveled from church to the mission site, we played a different parent leading devotions and praying over the students. The students loved it. It is also a good way to take your senior pastor with you if he can't go on the youth trip. Familiar voices are encouraging on a long trip.

Hope Prather

→→SENIOR SHARE TIME→→→→

The last night of our senior high mission trip is a worship service led by the seniors. We stay at a church away from the work camp site after we've completed our camp. The underclassmen begin by sharing their favorite memories of the seniors on mission trips or their past mission trip memories. This can be quite hilarious and at times may need to be censored.

Next, the seniors put together some type of skit about their favorite memories, and each of them passes on words of wisdom. They express what the youth group has done for them. We then have praise and worship with communion served by our seniors. We all cry and share our love for Christ with each other. It is almost impossible to bring the youth down off this mountaintop experience and get them to sleep that night.

The best witness to the impact of this service are the adults who'd complained all day about why we didn't just go home instead of being on the road an extra night. By the time the service is over, they are thanking God for the opportunity to

...THE SENIORS PUT TOGETHER SOME TYPE OF SKIT ABOUT THEIR FAVORITE MEMORIES, AND EACH OF THEM PASSES ON WORDS OF WISDOM.

witness these young adults sharing their faith journey with everyone.

Mary Anne Waldrip

→→ROAD MYSTERY→→→→

I do a road rules kind of thing each year with my seniors. I don't tell them where we're going; they just show up with their luggage. They get an envelope with a clue for the first day. They submit guesses, and we head there. If it's a road trip, we hop in the van and go. If it is a plane trip we go to the airport. At each stop they have a chore or assignment to complete to get points. I also randomly make up things to give them more points or to maintain order.

They get points for correct guesses and completed assignments. At the end of the trip the person with the most points wins a personal dorm-sized refrigerator. Here are samples from two trips.

TRIP ONE

From Dallas to the Oklahoma City Federal Building Memorial

To Kansas to Colorado

In Colorado a Denver stop for a downtown adventure game

Lake Dillon stop for a bike ride around a mountain lake

To a mountain cabin

To River Rafting adventure trip

To Royal Gorge Bridge adventure

To Colorado Springs with tons of cool things to do

To road trip home

I DON'T TELL THEM WHERE WE'RE GOING; THEY JUST SHOW UP WITH THEIR LUGGAGE. THEY GET AN ENVELOPE WITH A CLUE FOR THE FIRST DAY.

ROAD HINTS

TRIP TWO (EACH STOP IS ONE DAY)

Fly to New York

Drive to Niagara Falls (stop one)

Drive to Hershey, Pennsylvania (stop two)

Drive to Philadelphia (stop three)

Drive to Washington, D.C. (stop four)

Drive to New York City (two-day stop)

Drive to Albany (fly home)

Our seniors love the trip, and they can't wait for it each year. The road mystery is a blast because no one knows where we're going. It's great!

Ted Blair

SOME KIDS HAVE NEVER BEEN ON AN OLD-FASHIONED FAMILY VACATION, AND ONE LIKE THIS CAN HELP THE GROUP BOND.

➤➤THE FAMILY TRIP➤➤➤➤

While on a trip last summer, we stopped to eat in Corbin, Kentucky, at the original Kentucky Fried Chicken restaurant. From this I got the idea to take the group on a family road trip. Do not take anything larger than a 15-passenger van and 4 sponsors. Throw in a couple of sponsors' kids for flavor—you know, the pesky little brother or sister. Give each student a disposable camera for pictures.

Plan your route with an amusement park or a national park as your final destination. Research quick stops along the way, such as restaurants that are not chains. It's okay to stop at a place that's the largest, original, or a youth group tradition. If you can't eat at such a restaurant in your area, stop at historical markers or other weird things. Some kids have never been on an old-fashioned family vacation, and one like this can help the group bond. This can be an excellent way to draw in some fringe kids.

Meriam Bull

→→TRIP SKITS

On our annual kick-off camping and rafting weekend trips, we have surprise skit bags made up for each van filled with youth. The groups open the bags once they are on the road and think up skits on the way up to the retreat area. They are given one hour on the second day to fine-tune details, and on the third day they present skits just before we start back home.

The adult judges vote on three categories: 1) creativity, 2) scriptural basis, and 3) use of all group members. Prizes are awarded and the skits are presented in the worship service the following few weeks. Everyone wins as they hear the Word of God presented in such a creative way. The youth gain experience being in front of the congregation, and the congregation sees that the trip was more than just camping or rafting.

Each bag has seven or eight items. All bags have three items that are the same (one of these is a Bible). The other items are all different. The crazier and more creative you are, the better. Items can be anything you can find around your home (that will fit in the bag), ranging from a small box of raisins or empty plastic Easter eggs to clothes hangers, fast food toys, baby rattles, and bean bag toys.

We're always amazed and inspired by the depth of our youths' spirit as they search to find God's Word in the most unusual places.

Sandy Teska and Sue Kanipe

→→SECRET PLAN→→→→

Find a sports complex (or arcade) on the way to your destination that has a miniature golf course, driving range, batting cages, et cetera. (Call a local church for suggestions, or use on-line yellow pages.) You might want to make the stop seem spontaneous, then offer to pay for everyone to golf. (Build this into your trip budget from the start.) The stop gets everyone out of the car so

FIND A

SPORTS

COMPLEX

(OR ARCADE)

ON THE WAY

TO YOUR

DESTINATION

THAT HAS A

MINIATURE

GOLF

COURSE,

DRIVING RANGE,

BATTING

CAGES,

ET CETERA.

ROAD
HINTS

they're not cranky; and if done well, it provides a great group bonding experience.

Jeff Dyer

→→DON'T GET COMFORTABLE→→→→

Every time our van stops on a road trip, everyone rotates seats so that they get to know each other a little better. Oh yeah, no headphones either! This helps our group jell a little bit more every time we leave the church.

Matt Reedy

→→CHANGE→→→→

This works best in a bus, not a van. Have kids change seats in an organized pattern every half hour. At each stop announce which seat is the winner. The person in that seat gets a free lunch or something.

Justin Miller

DON'T TRY TO
FOLLOW
EACH OTHER
TO YOUR
DESTINATION.
SOME
DRIVERS
WILL ALWAYS
DRIVE FASTER
OR SLOWER THAN
EVERYONE
ELSE.

→→SERVICE STATION SERVANTHOOD→→→→

During your road trip make sure you travel with latex gloves, all-purpose cleaner, sponges, toilet brushes (anything you might need to clean bathrooms). Cleaning bathrooms gives us a tangible way to share the love of Christ and serve the towns we travel through. In addition to cleaning bathrooms, we carry small business cards with us that explain our service and thank people for the opportunity to serve them. This on-the-road service project provides your youth an opportunity to be blessed by serving others.

Text from business card: Thank you for allowing us to serve you today. May you feel the love of God today. In Christ, _____
(youth group name)

James Riddle

→→PAY IT BACKWARD

I work with the junior high youth group at our church, and every time we cross a bridge on a trip the lead car pays for all the cars in our group and then some. The junior highers love to see the reactions of the people and talk about the conversations that might be going on in those cars when they learn that someone else has paid the price for them. What a great segue...

Kelly Haynes

→→WHERE ARE WE GOING AGAIN?→→→→

Don't laugh. You'd be surprised. There are followers and there are leaders. Some followers WANT to be leaders. Some leaders cannot lead. Make sure every driver in your caravan has detailed directions. You can get turn-by-turn directions from www.mapquest.com. Provide maps for each driver.

Don't try to follow each other to your destination. Some drivers will always drive faster or slower than everyone else. Drivers who buzz the yellow light can separate a group indefinitely.

→→KNOW YOUR DRIVERS→→→→

Some insurance companies require a list of all drivers who participate in church events. Get photocopies of each driver's license. You may want to create a form for each driver that says that they have not had any traffic violations for the last year. The form could also include a statement that says, "I will obey all traffic laws." Then have each driver sign the form.

Even if your drivers are just volunteering this one time, they are ministers. Be sure they know they are being watched. They are role models. Their behavior is being studied and modeled.

EVEN IF YOUR DRIVERS ARE JUST VOLUNTEERING THIS ONE TIME, THEY ARE MINISTERS.

ROAD HINTS

→→CHOOSE A MEETING SPOT→→→→

When you pass out directions to the drivers, choose a meeting spot in advance. Say something like, "We'll stop at the first McDonald's past exit 19."

If someone gets lost, at least they know where the rest of the group will be.

→→CELL PHONES→→→→

Have one in every vehicle.

→→PERMISSION SLIPS→→→→

Keep the originals of all permission slips with you. Make your drivers copies for those teens who ride in their cars. Permission slips should always include emergency phone numbers of parents, all necessary insurance information, and a signature from a parent giving you permission to administer emergency medical treatment.

→→SAME TEENS, SAME CARS→→→→

Be sure your teens know that they are not to switch cars at rest stops. The car you start out in is the car you will arrive in. Volunteer drivers have enough to worry about without thinking they left someone behind.

→→WHERE'S KRISTIN?→→→→

Tell all drivers to do a head count before pulling out of the parking lot. It only takes a second, and you won't leave anyone behind. Don't laugh. It happens. (See: Horror Stories)

→→FOOD→→→→

You can set a blanket policy regarding all vehicles in the trip. However, the best policy is that the driver rules. If someone has graciously volunteered to drive for your road trip let her be

IF SOMEONE HAS GRACIOUSLY VOLUNTEERED TO DRIVE FOR YOUR ROAD TRIP LET HER BE IN CHARGE OF HER CAR.

in charge of her car. If a driver doesn't want soda pop and french fries eaten in the car, then that's the rule. Make sure both students and drivers know that the driver is the ultimate authority.

➤➤COMMUNION➤➤➤➤

One of the greatest things we do on a road trip (especially while returning home from a weekend retreat) is to stop along the way and have an impromptu communion service. Rather than have communion at the last service or meeting, we saved it for a scenic spot on the way home. Of course the teens didn't know about it, but the leaders did. It helps if the van drivers know it's coming!

We brought a loaf of French bread, some grape juice, and some small cups with us (some hand sanitizer wouldn't hurt). One year we stopped at a scenic overlook. Another year, it was at a spot where a river ran beside the highway. The point is to create the right moment, not necessarily the right location.

I'll read 1 Corinthians 11:23-26, explain what communion means to me, then serve them. Sometimes we sing, other times we have a debriefing time to share what God showed us on the trip or retreat. Either way, it's a positive experience. Once our kids started expecting it, we had to change strategies.

Jon Perrin and Doug Combs

➤➤TWO-WAY DEVOTIONS➤➤➤➤

While traveling, you can share devotions among vehicles. You need two-way radios that are set on the same channel for each vehicle. The leader initiates devotions while on the road. It is important to make sure there is a Bible in each

BEFORE THE TRIP, MAKE A CHALK MARK ON THE SIDE OF THE FRONT RIGHT TIRE OF THE BUS OR VAN WITH NAMES (OR SEAT NUMBERS.)

vehicle. Ask each vehicle to read Scripture; then ask questions about the reading. Each vehicle discusses questions independently first, then as a whole group.

To make it more interesting, give each vehicle a code name or let them create their own. Middle schoolers and senior high students both get into this type of devotion.

John Brookshire

⇢⇢THE WINNER IS...⇢⇢⇢⇢

Before the trip, make a chalk mark on the side of the front right tire of the bus or van with names (or seat numbers). When the bus or van stops, the leader looks at the front tire to see the name that's closest to the pavement. This person gets a prize, gets to choose where you stop for lunch, or gets to stand in line first at the ice cream stop. Make it something fun and positive.

Brent Thomas

⇢⇢BATHROOM BREAKS⇢⇢⇢⇢

Inform the teens that you will take scheduled bathroom stops. "I didn't have to then" is not an acceptable excuse. By their teen years they should be pretty well acquainted with their own bladder capacity. Buying a soda pop that is so large it has its own tide is not a good idea. Set a rule that anyone who can't hold it must pay a dollar to the youth mission fund. Keep an envelope in the glove compartment for just such an emergency.

⇢⇢ZIPLOC BAGS⇢⇢⇢⇢

Some people are not natural born travelers. Sometimes, "Pull over now!" is not enough time. Keep the gallon size Ziplocs on hand for kids who get queasy.

BUYING A SODA POP THAT IS SO LARGE IT HAS ITS OWN TIDE IS NOT A GOOD IDEA.

THE JOURNAL

Take along a blank notebook and allow everyone to write in the book every day of the trip. They can keep a diary of what's going on, write poems, or draw pictures. They can write in the journal any time they feel like it.

POSTCARDS FROM THE EDGE

Before you leave on a road trip, cut poster board into postcard-sized rectangles. Print out address labels with names of your senior pastor, members of the board, and any student who didn't get to come on the road trip. Put stamps on the postcards, and bring them with you. The trick here is to have a hundred or more postcards. This will run you an astounding 22 bucks in postage. Pass out postcards at any opportunity. Five or six cards should go into a mailbox at every rest stop. Have your students draw pictures of the things they see on the trip and write a few sentences on the back.

JOE'S GARAGE

See if the group members can find a business or street with their names. If you have time, stop and take a picture of the individuals in front of their businesses.

WINDOW ART

Use the van windows to create great works of art. Dry-erase markers easily wipe off the glass. Colored cellophane, cut into shapes, can turn the van windows into stained glass windows. Be sure the driver's view is not blocked.

ORDER GROUP FOOD

A great way to build group unity is to sit students all at one table and order plates of group

USE THE VAN WINDOWS TO CREATE GREAT WORKS OF ART. DRY ERASE MARKERS EASILY WIPE OFF THE GLASS.

food. Fill the table with appetizers. Italian and Chinese restaurants are good about bringing giant platters to the table. I once took a group into McDonald's where the special was two cheeseburgers and two fries for two bucks. I went up to the counter and said, "I'd like forty of that special." We took bags of burgers and fries back to the church and just laid it all out on the table. The supper table is a wonderful place for laughter and conversation. It's a great opportunity for a group to jell.

→→KEEP THE HANDS BUSY→→→→

There's an old saying that you can say things while doing the dishes that you can't say at the dinner table. Something about having busy hands makes conversation easier. Prior to the trip buy some fun cheap toys (try www.ustoyco.com), and pass them out at the beginning of each day. They will wind up in the strangest places, but when you sit down to debrief at the end of each day, the lines of communication open more easily because the fingers are busy.

→→IN THE DARK→→→→

Nighttime travel hours are a great time to get kids talking. With nothing to look at out the window, it's amazing how introspective teenagers can be after a long day and hours to go before they sleep.

→→THINGS THAT GO "FRRRRRRRRP" IN THE NIGHT→→→→

Convenience stores often offer large drinks and loooooooong straws. If you take a long straw and place one end in your mouth and one end in your armpit and then blow you will get a nice flatulent sound. You can adjust this sound by tightening

...IT'S

AMAZING

HOW

INTROSPECTIVE

TEENAGERS

CAN BE AFTER

A LONG DAY

AND HOURS

TO GO BEFORE

THEY SLEEP.

and relaxing your armpit. Here's the setup:
Practice this art at home.

One night of the trip, as you all try to sleep on
a church floor someplace, begin to act as if you're
angry. Yell a few times about unnecessary noise.
After the lights go out remove the straw from
under your pillow and play a single "note." Yell
something like, "All right, knock it off!" See how
long it takes your kids to figure out where the
noise comes from.

→→AND DON'T FORGET...

When you create permission slips, write down
in detail the exact directions to your destination.
Then include a line just before the parent signature that says:

> I understand that I may be called upon to retrieve
> my child if his or her behavior should become an
> obstacle to the rest of the trip.

There are three rules of discipline that
should appear on every permission slip and be
read aloud at every pre-trip meeting. They are
as much a guideline for the trip leader as for
student. Once they're learned, they must be
enforced, or they'll be worthless. (This is where
being a youth minister stops being fun.)

Rule #1: If your behavior negatively affects
the trip (e.g., continuous disrespect, leaving the
group), you will be taken aside by the youth
leader privately and told your unacceptable
behavior must change immediately.

Rule #2: If #1 doesn't work, you and the
youth leader will call your parents to explain
what you're doing and come up with a solution.

Rule #3: If #2 doesn't work, you and the youth
leader will call your parents and ask them to pick
you up, regardless of the time of day or how many
days are left on the trip.

YELL SOMETHING LIKE "ALL RIGHT, KNOCK IT OFF!" SEE HOW LONG IT TAKES YOUR KIDS TO FIGURE OUT WHERE THE NOISE COMES FROM.

ROAD HINTS

...WHEN ONE PERSON IS ALLOWED TO RUIN THE EXPERIENCE FOR OTHERS AND CONTINUES TO DO SO AFTER REPEATED WARNINGS, SOMETIMES YOU HAVE TO CUT THEM LOOSE TO TEACH THEM A LESSON.

About the three rules of discipline:

Be ready to enforce them. This is hard. Nobody wants to be the bad guy, but sometimes it's necessary.

In my 15 years of youth ministry I've reached Rule #2 about six or eight times. I've reached Rule #3 only twice. Both times it resulted in heavy embarrassment for the student (and the parent) and an extra meeting with the senior pastor, but when one person is allowed to ruin the experience for others and continues to do so after repeated warnings, sometimes you have to cut them loose to teach them a lesson. Maybe they can behave on the next trip.

CHAPTER

HORROR STORIES

OOPS! I DID IT AGAIN.

We took our kids to Alaska for a mission trip. Part of our sightseeing was to drive to Seward, Alaska, about 3 hours from our lodge in Anchorage. On the way back we stopped at Exit Glacier, one of the big ice fields in Alaska and about 30 miles from Seward. When my vehicle got to Exit Glacier, the first van had already unloaded, and our group was in the line at the restrooms. I didn't see David, one of our chaperones, so I assumed he was in the port-a-potty. I started slapping the walls and door saying, "Is everything coming out alright?" and "Don't

I STARTED **SLAPPING** THE **WALLS** AND **DOOR** SAYING, "IS EVERYTHING COMING OUT **ALRIGHT?"**

fall in." You guessed it—it wasn't David, and the guy inside was not too impressed with me. Oops.

We looked for David and realized we'd left him in Seward—alone, in the dark. One of the adults left to find him, and by the time he found David, David had already walked and jogged about 5 miles toward Anchorage. Oops.

To make matters worse, David told one of our kids when he went to the restroom (in Seward) and told her not to leave him—the kid never told us. Oops.

Tim and Tasha Levert

→→LOSING IT ALL ON THE RAPIDS→→→→

When I tried to save one of my kids from falling into the New River in West Virginia, I threw myself into the river as I pulled her up. As I went over a small, 80-feet deep waterfall area, I was pulled under and could not see the light. I finally ran out of air and gave up.

Eventually I floated to the top. The kids thought I had drowned, but when they saw me surface, they brought the raft to me. I didn't have much strength left. When they tried to help me in, we had to stop suddenly because I realized I'd lost my shorts. After debating how to handle the situation, I reached down and found the shorts snagged on my sandals. The story is longer, but this gives you an idea of what happened.

The two most common quotes were: "Check out that big white moon!" and "Boy, pull your britches on!"

Scott Miller

WHEN THEY TRIED TO HELP ME IN, WE HAD TO STOP SUDDENLY BECAUSE I REALIZED I'D LOST MY SHORTS.

→→LOST! (IN THE VAN)→→→→

Our youth group carpooled in three parents' vans to a DC Talk and Michael W. Smith concert two hours away. Jordan, a small sixth grade student, sat in front a giant speaker for the entire concert and developed a huge headache. When the concert ended, we stopped and got her some headache medicine. The conversion van she rode in had a bed in the back, and she fell asleep during the two-hour ride home. We arrived back at the church at 1 a.m. The kids went home with their families, and the vans were returned to the appropriate parents' homes.

At 4 a.m. I got a call from a frantic mom asking, "Where is my daughter?" I calmed her down, and we replayed the scenario—concert, headache, medicine, drive home. We could only figure that Jordan must still be asleep in the back of the borrowed conversion van.

I got dressed and drove to that home, fully expecting to find Jordan asleep in the back. I was shocked to find she was not there! I drove to the church to look for her there. Along the route Jordan's parents stopped me. They had her in the car with them and explained that she woke up in the van, got out, did not know where she was, and just started walking! She walked to a 24-hour grocery and called her parents. I don't know why that family left our church! It was a horror story at the time, but it's hilarious now.

Bill Smith

→→CARRYING THE CASE →→→→

My first retreat away from the church was the junior high fall retreat. We were only going an hour and a half from the church. However, the middle section of my tail pipe fell off halfway to the camp. The only place to stop within 15 miles was a local bar. One of the other sponsors and I went into the bar to call the church for help. No one answered the phones at the church so we went with Plan B. Ten minutes later we walked out of the bar with beer cases as the youths watched.

WE COULD **ONLY FIGURE** THAT JORDAN MUST **STILL BE ASLEEP** IN THE **BACK** OF THE BORROWED CONVERSION **VAN.**

0.6

The comments were as unreal as the contents of the cases. We used the thin cases to handle the hot tail pipe that fell off and stored it inside the bus. During all of this, one youth managed to take a picture of us carrying the beer cases. That picture made its way around the church, and we later had to explain the true scenario.

Rev. Owen Skinner

→→U-HAULS AND
DRIVE THRUS→→→→

I was the new youth minister, nervous and excited, heading to my first Passport summer camp in Daytona, Florida. I was the only adult on the trip who had not been to camp with this group before. I was also driving a U-Haul for the first time.

We had some extra time, so we stopped to clean out our vans. I pulled my van straight up to the trash bin at a Burger King without thinking about how difficult it would be to get the U-Haul out of that spot. I tried to go straight back—not easy for anyone with a U-Haul on a 15-passenger van, especially a rookie. It didn't work. Then I had a brilliant idea. I would just turn around and drive the U-Haul through the drive thru window space. It would be a tight squeeze, but I knew it would go. My kids would think I was so cool if I pulled it off!

I turned into the drive thru and waited for the other customers to give their orders. I started to pull forward and realized that my U-Haul was getting wedged between the building and wall on its opposite side. That's right, I was stuck in the Burger King drive thru with 15 kids and a 6 by 12 U-Haul that was loaded from ceiling to floor with suitcases!

Cars piled up behind us, my adult chaperones were furious, my kids were all laughing at me—it was terrible. I asked another adult to help get me

I STARTED TO
PULL
FORWARD
AND REALIZED
THAT MY
U-HAUL WAS
GETTING
WEDGED
BETWEEN THE
BUILDING
AND WALL
ON ITS
OPPOSITE SIDE.

out of the space because she had driven one before. She refused! I flipped out—what if my authority with the kids never recovers from this incident? What if my adults call the church deacons before we get back to tell them how crazy they were to hire such a moron?

Then, like a messenger from heaven, one of the older youths who really hadn't warmed up to me, got out of the other van and offered his help. Several other boys piled out of the vans to offer their muscle and their trailer-hauling know-how. Several of us unhooked the U-Haul, while the others cheered us on and took pictures to capture the moment. A small committee was elected to politely explain to the Burger King manager why the drive thru business had suddenly gone bust.

We pushed the U-Haul back to a space that we could get the van into—all together, as a group. I watched several of my kids take charge while others comforted and encouraged me. We shared funny stories about similar situations.

What started out a nightmare turned into a great bonding experience for the kids and me. My advice for road trips is: when you take a U-Haul, be very careful about where you try to get it in and out of. Also, watch the person at the rental place hook the thing up so you know how to unhook it in a pinch.

Rev. Johnny Lewis

→→BRRRRR→→→

Each year in February our youth group attends one of Canada's largest youth conventions at Briercrest Bible College in Saskatchewan. As 40 of us left the church parking lot outside of Vancouver, British Columbia, excited about what was in store, nothing could have prepared us for the 24-hour bus ride ahead.

The trip began routinely enough aboard our luxury tour bus until about four hours into our

AS 40 OF US LEFT THE CHURCH PARKING LOT OUTSIDE OF VANCOUVER, BRITISH COLUMBIA, EXCITED ABOUT WHAT WAS IN STORE, NOTHING COULD HAVE PREPARED US FOR THE 24-HOUR BUS RIDE AHEAD.

journey. That was when it began to get a little cold. We asked the driver to turn up the heat, and he let us know it was as high as possible. This was the first sign of trouble ahead. The temperature was slightly below freezing when we left, and we knew as we headed east toward the Rockies it would get much colder.

Ten hours into our trip, the inside windows had half an inch of ice on them so we couldn't see outside. The driver had an eight-inch hole he could peer through to see the road. The pennies we stuck on the windows became encased in the ice like a coin collection; pop, juice, water or contact lens solution froze inside the bus. The temperature inside the bus was now 28 degrees Fahrenheit. We wanted to stop to thaw, but our driver, despite having no feeling in his feet, did not want to stop the bus for fear of the gears freezing up. After all of this we still had ten hours to go.

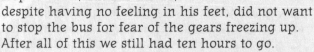

Finally after beginning to feel as if we were going to become another story like the movie *Alive*, we arrived at our destination and had a great time growing in our relationships with each other and Jesus. The bus we were in had arrived from California the day before, and it had not been prepared for a cold Canadian winter. Thankfully the heat was fixed for our ride home to the wet but warmer West Coast.

Allan Rempel

→→MOVING THE GROUP→→→→

A few years ago our youth group went on a trip into the desolate Florida panhandle. As we headed home about 7 p.m. on Saturday night, one of our two vans died. A half hour west of

WE **COULDN'T** **REPAIR** OUR VAN, WE COULDN'T **RENT** ANOTHER VAN, AND **NONE** OF THE **CHURCHES** IN THE AREA WOULD **LOAN** OR RENT US **ONE OF THEIRS.**

Tallahassee is no place to be stranded because nothing is open on a Saturday night.

We couldn't repair our van, we couldn't rent another van, and none of the churches in the area would loan or rent us one of theirs. It would take nearly three hours for someone to come get us. So what did we do?

We went to U-Haul and rented a moving truck for $19.95. The girls got in the remaining van, and all of the guys got in the back of the U-Haul with the luggage. We pulled down the sliding door and gave them a hearty, "See ya back in Ocala!"

For the next 3 hours, they had World Wrestling entertainment in the pitch-black darkness of that U-Haul truck. ($19.95! What a great price for rental transportation—we should do all of our trips like this!)

James A. Hull

→→DON'T DRINK THE RIVER WATER →→→→

When I was on the other end of youth ministry as a student, I went on an eight-week outreach program called Summer Servants. We spent one week in the bottom of the Grand Canyon sharing Christ with the Havasupi people. With scorching heat and hikes as long as 12 miles, somehow sooner or later most of us got a mouthful of river water.

Apparently a parasite that lives in the water takes a few days to kick in. Once it does, you're pretty much bound to the bathroom for a few days as your body tries to rid itself of these parasites out "one end or the other." It started to affect us on the two-day bus drive to our next destination. Much of this drive was through the barren Nevada and Arizona desert (not a lot of restrooms along the road—or even a tall bush, for that matter). The bus had to stop every 15 minutes while someone jumped out with a roll of T.P. and

WITH SCORCHING HEAT AND HIKES AS LONG AS 12 MILES, SOMEHOW SOONER OR LATER MOST OF US GOT A MOUTHFUL OF RIVER WATER.

a couple faithful friends held a privacy blanket. That really added interest to the trip! Sometimes four or more had to stop at once.

My favorite part was when I sat toward the back of the bus with someone who had her feet up on the seat by the window. Out of the blue something splattered on her feet. Thinking someone had dumped some ice out the window she gave a satisfied, "Ahhhhhh" from the cool refreshment on her hot feet. But then (you guessed it), she discovered what hit her feet was someone losing his cookies out one of the front windows of the bus at 55 mph. None of this is recommended, but it does add considerable excitement to an otherwise boring trip.

Josh Lieurance

→→A LONG TRIP→→→→

My wife and I began our youth ministry summer trip experience with an exciting road trip to Dallas, Texas. It was our first year in ministry, and we had grand plans. We took about 22 members of our youth group and staff to the Youth for the Nations conference, almost one thousand miles away from our home in Pierre, South Dakota. We planned to use our 43-passenger tour bus, but we found out it needed a replacement engine part two days before our planned departure. Yes, two days! Needless to say, we went ballistic when we heard the news.

We ended up asking our church members for help. In other words, we begged them for their vehicles. My parents donated their Suburban, and another family donated their jeep. We finally talked another member into letting us use a Suburban, and another let us pull their trailer behind one of the Suburbans to carry our luggage. It would be a tight fit, but it would do—almost.

The day before we left, the second Suburban we'd lined up was on its way back with a group of our young children from a children's camp. It broke down and wouldn't be fixed in time for us to use. Hmmmm... This was getting difficult.

My wife and I wanted to give up, but our pastor was the hero and saved us from canceling the trip. He found out that his neighbors had just purchased a fifteen-passenger van, and they would loan it to us at no cost! Whew! What an unexpected blessing.

MURPHY'S LAW

The day of the trip, we realized how important the extra seats in the extended cab van were. We barely fit in all our junk and luggage. The trailer was loaded to the ceiling from front to back. You could really feel the added weight when driving the Suburban.

Before we left the state, our girls stepped on the Suburban's running board and broke it off. Neither the girl nor we felt very good (smile) about that. We just hoped Mom and Dad wouldn't be too upset. We picked it up and shoved it into the already-too-full trailer.

It was smooth sailing for the next thousand miles. We had radio communication between the vehicles, so every once in a while, we had to listen to lame jokes and irritating riddles from our travel-weary teenagers. We planned to get to the conference early to make sure we had the best dorm rooms and got registration taken care of before the crowds showed up. It was a nice thought.

After about nineteen hours on the road and about one hour away from our destination, the leaf spring on the trailer gave out. We, of course, were in heavy traffic on a Dallas Interstate. I was driving the Suburban, and I noticed smoke coming from the rear of the vehicle as I heard, "Pull over! Pull over!" coming though my radio. My wife witnessed the trailer tire being ripped to shreds as we rolled on. Miraculously, I somehow got off the Interstate and made it to the first exit.

AFTER ABOUT NINETEEN HOURS ON THE ROAD AND ABOUT ONE HOUR AWAY FROM OUR DESTINATION, THE LEAF SPRING ON THE TRAILER GAVE OUT.

0.6

We herded the kids out of the vehicles to sit and enjoy the July Texas sun. Our pastors, who were along to help drive, had already left the group to find a place where they would stay for the week. We called them on the cell phone and told them what happened, and they were on their way to help. One adult volunteer stayed with the trailer and our pastor to put it in storage for the evening until it could be fixed. We trekked on with the same two vehicles, PLUS all of the luggage from the trailer. To be quite honest, it was not a pleasant hour.

When we arrived at the camp, we got registered and checked in with no problems. The guys unloaded their luggage at their dorm rooms, and the girls took the van over to unload theirs. An hour later, I found out that the van was stalled at the front entrance of the girls' dormitory! Our most mechanically gifted teen couldn't fix the problem, so we pushed it into a corner of the parking lot.

I and the only other male adult volunteer spent the week replacing the leaf spring on the trailer and calling the fix-it station that was working on the van. First, they couldn't find a part, so we drove to the nearest Dodge dealer, purchased the part, and gave it to them. We called often to ask why we didn't see anyone working on the van when we drove by. Third, camp ended, and the van still wasn't fixed. We took our teens to the station's waiting area in shifts. Suddenly, they worked really fast to get our van fixed. We were on the road within the hour.

Our teenagers experienced a life-changing week. Many received a calling on their lives and many live differently now because of that trip. It was God-ordained, no doubt. I just didn't understand all of it at the time. That trip glued us all together. I just wish we hadn't had to deal with all of the "ungluing" in the process!

Pastor Shawn M. Shoup

AN HOUR
LATER, I
FOUND OUT
THAT THE
VAN WAS
STALLED
AT THE FRONT
ENTRANCE
OF THE GIRLS'
DORMITORY!

⟶LUNCH SNATCHER⟶

While taking my kids to camp one summer, we made our traditional stop at McDonald's. The whole herd piled out of the van and into the restaurant to get lunch. As I waited to order, one of my youth came up to me and said that a woman was eating his food.

At first I thought that he was joking (which tends to happen occasionally), but then I realized that this young man was really upset to the point of tears. I looked at him and then looked at the woman as she sat there among the other youth eating his Big Mac. I gave him some money and told him to get back in line to get another Big Mac, and I walked over to talk with this Big-Mac-stealing woman.

I said to her, "I think there must have been some confusion (giving her the benefit of the doubt)." She replied, "What do you mean?" I said, " Well you're eating that young man's Big Mac." She looked me straight in the eye and said, "I didn't see his name on it."

Then she took another bite and continued to look me right in the eye. I was so taken aback by her response that I turned and walked away. As we finished our meal the woman got up to use the restroom. When she did, she left a paper sack sitting on the floor where she was sitting. I know it probably wasn't the best thing to do, but I had everyone get in the van as fast as possible. As soon as they were in the van, I walked over and picked up her bag. As I headed for the door, she saw me, and we both took off in a sprint. I jumped in the driver's seat and locked the door. This woman began to scream and pound on the hood of the van. Everyone in the parking lot stared at us as we pulled off. And in the bag, as we headed for the interstate, we saw something I will never forget. In that bag was a pile of bologna—just like this whole story has been a pile of bologna.

Josh Donaldson

> I LOOKED AT HIM AND THEN LOOKED AT THE WOMAN AS SHE SAT THERE AMONG THE OTHER YOUTH EATING HIS BIG MAC.

HORROR STORIES

PARKING GARAGES

When you take a youth group to a convention, it's important to park close to the hotel. Parking in the hotel's parking garage is ideal. However, remember that the height restrictions include the height of the car topper! Yes, it's true—I drove right into the roof of the parking garage, knocked the car topper right off the top of the van. My kids thought this was absolutely hilarious, even though their clothes were strewn across the garage floor.

David L. Marvin

→→HEAT AND AIR CONDITIONING→→→→

A couple of summers ago, our youth group traveled around to perform a musical. We packed up three vans and a U-Haul and headed south from Ohio. We rented one 15-passenger van that had air conditioning for only the driver, no carpet, and bare metal sides.

The trip went okay until the temperature went over 100 degrees. It was bathing suits and sweat all over. We arrived in Alabama and decided this was not going to work. But what could we do?

The youth workers got together and devised a plan. First stop: Wal-Mart. We bought flexible dryer vent tubing, an end box, duct tape, and some tools. Then we stopped at a carpet store. They let us pick through the free remnants, and we found some nice shag. We got some very large pieces of cardboard, and headed back to the church where we were staying.

We pulled the seats out of the van and installed carpet. We wrapped the carpet pieces up the side to window height, and generously applied duct tape to the seams and sides.

Then we cut the vent tube and duct taped it over the two center air conditioning vents on

THEN WE CUT THE VENT TUBE AND DUCT TAPED IT OVER THE TWO CENTER AIR CONDITIONING VENTS ON THE DASHBOARD.

the dashboard. We ran the tubing up the front windshield and along the ceiling to the back, attaching it to the mirror and dome light fixtures with coat hangers and duct tape. We kept the cardboard along the sides to put on the windows when it got hot. After that, we wrestled the seats back in place.

And that is how you make homemade air conditioning! The youth group named the van Apollo 13. It was ugly, but it was definitely the coolest place to ride for the next two weeks.

Bob Mako

→→TRIP TO CAMP→→→→

Hey, this story sounds really crazy, but I promise it is true. It happened to my youth group when I was a teen more than 10 years ago—obviously before I was a youth leader or even knew I would be.

Our youth group began our annual road trip to summer youth camp. We met at the church at 6 a.m. and got on the road 30 minutes later. (Since we're charismatic, we believe in miracles!). Everyone in the van except the driver slept in heavenly bliss. About 45 minutes into the trip, we woke abruptly. We had a flat tire—in the middle of rush hour traffic! Our youth pastor and a couple of guys jumped out to fix it. No problem; fixed in about 10 minutes. We jumped back in and on we went!

About 2 1/2 hours later, in the smack dab middle of nowhere, guess what? Another flat tire! Oh no! That was our spare! Our youth pastor had to walk to the nearest town to buy a tire. He got there in 30 minutes and had to wait another 30 minutes for the shop to open—while the youth group sat stranded on the side of the highway, in the middle of nowhere. In July at 10 a.m. in Texas, heat is an understatement. While we waited, a huge chartered bus passed us and honked and

WHILE WE WAITED, A HUGE CHARTERED BUS PASSED US AND HONKED AND WAVED, BUT DIDN'T STOP TO OFFER HELP. IT WAS ANOTHER YOUTH GROUP FROM OUR DENOMINATION GOING TO THE SAME CAMP!

waved, but didn't stop to offer help. It was another youth group from our denomination going to the same camp!

Next, the van hauling the luggage trailer got a flat. Do you know how hard it is to find one of those small-sized tires? Next, our transmission began to leak, the van started smoking, and we had to drive 15 miles per hour for about half an hour. Finally, it rained!

What a horrible trip! But what an incredible experience we had with God at camp. The experience still influences my life to this day. We learned a valuable lesson on that trip—when the enemy presses in harder and harder until you feel you can't stand up to the resistance—keep going. You're going in the right direction, and you're doing something right!

Benjy Oliver

→→COUNTING HEADS→→→→

I once worked for a church located right across the street from a McDonald's. The night we were to leave for the Winter Retreat, about two dozen kids milled around in the parking lot. I took names, and after some last-minute packing changes, we loaded up to head out. Unbeknownst to me, two sisters had decided to walk across the street for a soda. We pulled away without them.

About an hour into the drive someone behind me said, "Where are Kristin and Megan?" I pulled over. We looked and sure enough, they weren't there. I borrowed a cell phone, called my senior pastor, and said, "I just left Kristin and Megan behind." He said, "I just happen to have Kristin and Megan's dad on the other line. Would you like to speak to him?" I said that I would not. Kristin and Megan's mom offered to drive the girls to the retreat center. Their father did not speak to me for a year.

UNBEKNOWNST TO ME, TWO SISTERS HAD DECIDED TO WALK ACROSS THE STREET FOR SODA. WE PULLED AWAY WITHOUT THEM.

ROAD GAMES

NOTHING HELPS PASS THE
time like a good road game. In this
section you'll find variations on classic
car games, games submitted by youth
workers from around the country, and
flat-out crazy originals that should
only be attempted by professionals.

→→POCKET SCAVENGER
HUNT→→→→

Create an in-the-vehicle scavenger
hunt. All items must come from pockets, the van floor, or purses. Some
sample items: lifesaver, straw, french
fry, pin, earring, driver's license, picture of a small child, one of each coin,
sock with a hole in it, cough drop, et
cetera. You can tailor the list based on
your group.

CREATE AN
IN-THE-VEHICLE
SCAVENGER
HUNT. ALL
ITEMS MUST
COME FROM
POCKETS,
THE VAN
FLOOR, OR
PURSES.

ROAD GAMES

➙➙CHALK IT UP➙➙

Take along a couple buckets of sidewalk chalk. At each stop along the way, including gas and food stops, use the chalk to make body outlines. The idea comes from the old movies that showed dead-body outlines on the ground. To make it ministry-oriented and a little less macabre, we used worship positions. Have students pose on the ground in praying positions of every sort. We had students holding hands and praising on the ground, and we used the chalk to outline their bodies. We also marked each spot with our youth group logo and a scripture reference. Then we took pictures of the students with their street art. It made our trip very memorable!

Sven Olson

> AT EACH STOP ALONG THE WAY, INCLUDING GAS AND FOOD STOPS, USE THE CHALK TO MAKE BODY OUTLINES.

➙➙ALL FIFTY STATES➙➙➙➙

Divide your group into two teams. Each team tries to spot license plates from as many different states as possible. Keep this game for the duration of the trip.

➙➙LICENSE PLATE SCRIPTURES➙➙➙➙

Since all good youth workers keep a Bible in their car (ahem), use the license plate to look up scripture verses. If a license plate reads LMD-2143 tell your students to look up chapter 21, verse 42 of the book of Luke, Matthew or Daniel. Make it a competition to see who can find it first. It's amazing to see how often the verse will actually fit with the situation at hand. Use this game to make a point of how God speaks to us all the time; we just have to listen.

➙➙FIND A WORD➙➙➙➙

See who in the group can be the first to come up with a word that includes all the letters in the spotted license plate. First, let the students use the letters in any order. After a while make it more difficult and require that the word use the letters in the order they are on the plate.

→→MAKE A SENTENCE

Use the letters on the license plate to create a sentence. GLD-368 could become God Likes Dogs.

→→CONVERSATIONS→→→→

Use the same principle as the previous game, but try to hold an actual conversation. HAY298 = How Are You? IBB476 = I've Been Better.

→→BOGGLE→→→→

Use the letters in a license plate as you would use the dice in the popular game Boggle. If the chosen plate has the letters LMP, give the riders 60 seconds to see how many words they can come up with that use all of those letters. Give half points to words that use two letters.

→→PLATE RUBBING→→→→

Take tracing paper along. When you stop for gas or the bathroom, have the kids see how many different states they can make license plate rubbings of. Be sure they ask the drivers for permission. Have a competition among the cars in your caravan.

→→HIGHWAY TWISTER→→→→

Use a traditional Twister spinner. Using masking tape cover the colors with phrases like "Right Window," "Rear Window," "Floor," and "Ceiling." This game is great in a church van.

WHEN YOU STOP FOR GAS OR THE BATHROOM, HAVE THE KIDS SEE HOW MANY DIFFERENT STATES THEY CAN MAKE LICENSE PLATE RUBBINGS OF.

STATE GOD 123

ROAD GAMES

→HONK IF YOU LOVE...

This game requires participation from fellow drivers so be mindful of your neighborhood before you play this game. Each player starts with fifty points. Each player should also have paper and markers or an erasable board. The object of the game is to reach 200 points first. Each player bets a certain number of points that they can make another driver honk their horn. The more obscure the item on the sign, the higher the point value.

For example, "Honk if you love cookies!" would be worth only a few points. "Honk if you love rubber donkey lungs" would be worth a higher point value. It is up to the rest of the group to agree on the amount of points awarded. The player then has three tries to make someone in another car honk.

●INSTRUCT THEM THAT FOR THE NEXT HOUR, NO ONE CAN COMMUNICATE EXCEPT BY STICKY NOTE.

→ NOBODY KNOWS →→→→

Each person chooses a little known fact that they believe nobody else will know. (Be sure they aren't choosing facts like "Where do I keep my skis?") Then group members ask their questions out loud, and they receive one point for each person they stump.

→→THE SOUND OF SILENCE →→→→

Hand everyone their own personal pad of sticky notes and a pen. Instruct them that for the next hour, no one can communicate except by sticky note. This is a great game to play when the driver needs some silence.

→→THE HUM GAME →→→→

Spend twenty or so miles with the rule that, when talking, you must say the word "hum" between words. "When hum are hum we hum going hum to hum stop hum for hum lunch?"

→→PUPPET SHOWS

This sounds silly, but it's really a blast. Pass out paper bags and markers. Make puppets and perform shows for other cars.

→→WHERE ARE WE GOING?→→→

First, check out a map of the route you'll take on your road trip. Pick out as many random names of cities, parks, museums...whatever. Then, make a list of them, and mix up the order. While your students check in and you're getting ready to take off, have the students put the places and names in the order that they think you'll pass them. When you take off, put up a map, and check off the places as you go. Make sure to have someone keep tabs. When you get to your destination (or even at stops along the way), figure out who got the correct order, or who was closest.

Jenny Pearson

→→HOW MUCH?→→→→

An hour or so before you stop for a road trip meal, figure out where you might stop, choose five or six menu items, and have each member of the group guess what the total bill will be for those items. Whoever gets closest without going over wins free breakfast from McDonald's (or whatever restaurant you go to).

It is especially fun if you get their guesses on videotape so that you can show the video later during the retreat.

Jennifer Barksdale

→→CHOSEN WORD→→→→

Introduce a new word on each day of the trip. It can be a word that students will not know, or

INTRODUCE A NEW WORD ON EACH DAY OF THE TRIP. IT CAN BE A WORD THAT STUDENTS WILL NOT KNOW, OR ONE THAT THEY DO KNOW AND WILL HAVE FUN WITH.

ROAD GAMES

one that they do know and will have fun with. Each day write the word (or print it out ahead of time) on a sheet of paper, and hang it inside each bus or each van. Encourage students to work that word into their conversations all day, every day. It will drive you crazy, but each day the students will look forward to the new word. For example, we used the word *plethora* one day. I never wanted to hear it again—yet I am reminded of that trip every time I hear it.

Hope Prather

⇢⇢TRACTORS⇢⇢⇢⇢

Split the group in half—left side and right side— to form two teams. Each team counts the number of tractors they see on their side of the road. If they see a graveyard on their side of the road, they lose all of their tractors. The team with the most tractors when you arrive at your destination wins.

Variation: If you don't have many tractors in your state, count the number of Starbucks you spot on each side of the road.

The driver can make the game interesting by detouring. It takes a little longer to get where you're going, but it's all about the game!

Brian Edwards

⇢⇢GAMES AND PRIZES⇢⇢⇢⇢

We go to Florida every summer with our youth. It is only an eight-hour ride, but I always have silly games to play with them to make it fun. I bring bags of candy for those who participate and cheap prizes for the winners. Make it stuff like Frisbees, water guns, beach balls, goggles, crayons, color books, cards, and yo-yos.

Some games everyone plays—like toilet paper relay, with both sides of the bus racing to pass the roll up and down the aisles until it is all unrolled.

...TOILET PAPER RELAY, WITH BOTH SIDES OF THE BUS RACING TO PASS THE ROLL UP AND DOWN THE AISLES UNTIL IT IS ALL UNROLLED.

Another one is to ask for random things such as the oldest penny, the most $1 bills, the first one to show me a picture of their mother or father, et cetera. Then I ask for several volunteers and put them in maybe three or four pairs. I use a stopwatch to time team members singing every other word of "Jesus Loves Me" or another song. The first person says *Jesus*; the second says *loves*; the first says *me*; and so on. Another game is to ask four or five people to tell you the 15th word in "The Star-Spangled Banner." Give prize to the one who says it first. Do this several times with different people using different songs. We once got about four people to put rubber gloves over their heads, cover their noses with the glove, and make it pop by blowing it up with their nose. This is really entertaining for the others on the bus.

Tonya
Tgo215@aol.com

→→GUESS THE MILES→→→→

Pass a form around for students to write their guesstimate of the exact number of miles the bus will travel on their journey. Give a clue and offer them guidelines to choose between (for example, somewhere between 56.5 miles and 89.2 miles). Make sure you record the exact mileage on the speedometer before you begin so you can award prizes later. Try to not have duplicate guesses.

David Furlong

→→THE COLOR GAME→→→→

Start with a color. Go around a circle as fast as you can for each person to name something that is that color. Allow no more than three seconds to think. If a person cannot name something, she is out of that round. Play until you have a winner for each color.

START
WITH A
COLOR.
GO AROUND A
CIRCLE AS
FAST AS YOU
CAN FOR
EACH
PERSON
TO NAME
SOMETHING
THAT IS
THAT
COLOR.

ROAD GAMES

→→RED OR BLACK →

Test each other's extra-sensory perception (ESP) abilities with a regular deck of cards. Hold up a card with the back facing a partner, and have him guess red or black. See who can get the most right.

→→THE NEARLY IMPOSSIBLE BUT EXCELLENT TIME FILLER CARD GAME →→→

Hold a shuffled deck of cards in your hand. Spell out O-N-E as you put a card from the top of the pile to the bottom of the pile. Turn the next card over. If it is an ace you win and move on to the number T-W-O.

→→PUNCH BUGGY→→→→

Many people have their own versions of this classic. Use this book to document the once-and-for-all-official rules to the game. Anytime a person sees a Volkswagen Beetle they can gently punch someone else in the arm and say, "punch buggy."

Once a punch buggy is used, another player, including the one who was punched, cannot use it again. There are no special rules for colors, new Beetles, or PT Cruisers.

→→JINX→→→→

Another classic that has varying rules. Here's a set of rules to go by in the event of conflicting ideas. If two people say the same word at the same time, one person may "jinx" the other player simply by saying the word "jinx". Physical contact is not necessary, but it's sometimes allowable. The "jinxed" player must then remain silent until someone else in the vehicle says his or her name.

IF TWO PEOPLE SAY THE SAME WORD AT THE SAME TIME, ONE PERSON MAY "JINX" THE OTHER PLAYER SIMPLY BY SAYING THE WORD "JINX."

LAST GAS

This one is gross but fun. If someone in the van breaks wind loudly, the others are then permitted to punch her in the arm repeatedly until she can say the name of three breakfast cereals.

CATCH THE WAVE

Divide the students into two groups. See how many people in other cars you can get to wave back at you. Each team gets one point for each waver. You can score multiple points if several people in one car wave. Set a time limit. If you are on a highway, be sure to give riders on both sides a chance to catch waves.

ALPHABET SENTENCE

See who can make the longest sentence using consecutive letters of the alphabet.

RESCUE HERO

Start off with a brief description of a princess locked in a tower guarded by a fire-breathing dragon. You can make a Shrek reference if you want. Have your kids find ways to rescue the princess using things they see outside the window. They need to cross the moat, find the princess, defeat the dragon, and get back across the moat.

CHAIN-CHAIN-CHAIN

Divide your students into two groups. The object of the game is to see which group can make the longest chain using only what is available to them in the vehicle. They can use belts, shoelaces, things they find on the floor of the van. When you pull into the next rest stop, measure the chains and see who wins.

THE OBJECT OF THE GAME IS TO SEE WHICH GROUP CAN MAKE THE LONGEST CHAIN USING ONLY WHAT IS AVAILABLE TO THEM IN THE VEHICLE.

ROAD GAMES

Tell the group you're going to give them a two-word clue. They need to come up with two more words that mean something similar to the clue, however their answers must rhyme. Here's an example: overweight bug = fat gnat. Got it?

Once you get through this list, have the group make up its own.

Clue	Answer
Inexpensive Off-Road Car	Cheap Jeep
Halt Broom	Stop Mop
Street Frog	Road Toad
False Pond	Fake Lake
Bug Sports Teacher	Roach Coach
Green Coin	Lime Dime
Sheriff In Charge	Top Cop
Sheep Soup	Ewe Stew
Night Song	Moon Tune
Skinny Pointer	Narrow Arrow
Cooked Detergent	Fried Tide
Bacon Jelly	Ham Jam
Little Glow	Slight Light
Grass Necklace	Weed Beads
Gaseous Frozen Treat	Burpy Slurpee
Stinky Savings and Loan	Rank Bank
Big Boat	Large Barge
Bug Injection	Beetle Needle
Sweet Snot	Sugar Booger

P..U!

THEY NEED TO COME UP WITH TWO MORE WORDS THAT MEAN SOMETHING SIMILAR TO THE CLUE, HOWEVER THEIR ANSWERS MUST RHYME.

Conjunction Tushy	But Butt
Smelly Finger	Stinky Pinky
Boy Snow	Male Hail
Operator's Flu	Please Hold Cold
Bad Gardener	Can't Plant
Ship Sweater	Boat Coat
Decayed Mucus	Snot Rot

⇢⇢BIZZ BUZZ⇢⇢⇢⇢

This classic game is always worth a good twenty minutes or so. Begin by going around the vehicle counting out loud in order 1, 2, 3, 4, 5, 6. When you get to the number seven they should say "Bizz" instead of the number. From this point on players must substitute any number that is a multiple of seven with the word "Bizz". If someone misses, they are not out (more than likely you have limited space and people). The person who fails to say "Bizz" at the proper time stays in the game and receives a point. You can start the game over at any time and add the word "Buzz" for multiples of five and "Bozz" for multiples of three.

⇢⇢FIVE SECONDS GAME⇢⇢⇢⇢

Choose a category and tell players they have five seconds to name five things in that category.

Examples:

Things you spread on toast

Keanu Reeves movies

Songs that have the word Love in the title

Things you can put ketchup on

Speed is the fun part of this game. Once one person fails to get the five things, immediately point to another person. Keep going until someone gets five, and then move on to the next category.

HAVE AN ADULT LEADER READ ONE OF THE LITTLE KNOWN FACTS AT RANDOM, AND SEE IF THE GROUP CAN GUESS WHOM THE MYSTERY PERSON IS.

ROAD GAMES

→ WHOZAT?

Pass out index cards and pencils. Have each person in the van write down three little-known things about themselves. Then have them pass the cards back. Have an adult leader read one of the little-known facts at random, and see if the group can guess who the mystery person is.

→ ONE MORE THAN YOU → → → →

Have two students face off against each other. (This works even if they aren't sitting beside each other.) Give them a category like soda pops. Have them take turns naming soda pops without repeating each other. Each player should have no more than ten seconds to come up with a name. If they can't name a product or if they repeat something already said, they are out of the game and the winner faces a new challenger. Try these categories to get started—breakfast cereals, car makers, radio stations, rock bands, green foods, and ways to cook potatoes.

PICK A
BILLBOARD
THAT YOU
DRIVE BY
AND SEE IF
YOUR GROUP
CAN USE
THE
SLOGAN ON
THE BILLBOARD
AS AN
ADVERTISEMENT
FOR GOD.

→ NAME THAT SPLAT → → → →

You need a sheet of thick poster board and some duct tape for this game. Secure the poster board to the front of the vehicle. Do not block the radiator. Leave the board there for the entire trip. During the trip, take the board and play "guess the bug" or cut it up as souvenirs for your students or cut it into squares and let the kids send them back to their parents as postcards.

→ BILLBOARDS → → → →

Pick a billboard that you drive by and see if

your group can use the slogan on the billboard as an advertisement for God. Give extra points if someone does it without changing a word of the slogan.

→→SELDOM-HEARD WORDS

Take a post-it note pad and write down bizarre, seldom-heard words. Pass these out at the beginning of the trip. Tell your students they must try to work their words into casual conversation. If a student thinks someone just used his secret word, he says so. The object of the game is to use your word without anyone knowing.

Here are some fun samples: Wonderbra, amphibian, bearded lady, euphoria, cartography, spinach, ellipsis, wholesale, Oxford, hillbilly, Zimbabwe, Mozambique, Katmandu, octogenarian, Beelzebub, phlebotomist, flautist, highfalutin, discombobulate, monotonous, melancholy, disillusion, debauchery, osculation, swank, brouhaha, catamaran, schnitzel, fandango, medulla oblongata, frankfurter, bongo, megaphone, Wankel rotary engine, juxtaposition, Duma, tomfoolery, shenanigans, ticktock, dazzle, bimonthly, and finite.

→→AFFIRMATION PING-PONG BALLS→→→→

Purchase a gross (144) of ping-pong balls. Use a marker to write the book, chapter, and verse number for affirming Scripture verses. Don't tell anyone you have these. See how creative you can be in planting these on your students. Slip them into pockets, book bags, and lunch bags.

After a day or so, pass them out to kids and have them leave them at rest stops, pay phones, and various other places for strangers to find.

PURCHASE

A GROSS OF

PING-
PONG
BALLS. USE
A MARKER
TO WRITE
THE BOOK,
CHAPTER,
AND VERSE
NUMBER FOR
AFFIRMING
SCRIPTURE
VERSES.

ROAD GAMES

→→JOHN WAYNE→→→

Have someone think of the name of a famous person. (Start with John Wayne.) The next person has to come up with a famous name that uses either John or Wayne in the first or last place. (Wayne Newton or Olivia Newton John) The next person can use any of the names the last person did. Keep going until someone gets stuck. Names cannot be repeated. You can establish rules of your own, such as they must be living persons or no people from your school.

→→DRAWBACK→→→

Have your group pair up in the van and take turns drawing pictures or spelling words—with their fingers, not their pens—on each other's backs. Then let them guess what the other person draws.

→→SHAVE AND A HAIRCUT→→→

This one is fun, but be aware of the neighborhood you're in. As you drive past someone, have a kid roll down the window and sing out, "Bum Ditty-um Bum," and see if the person responds with "Bum Bum." You can also do this with clapping.

→→ONE WORD→→→

Spend an entire hour speaking in only one-word sentences—slow speaking, but summing up the meaning in one word. Assign a penalty for anyone who says more than one word.

→→SNOWFLAKE NAPKINS→→→

Using only napkins you pick up from fast food establishments, see who can make the most unique snowflake. Use a folding process or make up your own.

CHAPTER  **thirteen**

DETOURS

SOMETIMES IN THE CONTEXT

of a Road Trip or Mission week it
becomes necessary to take a little vacation from reality. The following is a list
of mental detours that can lighten a
tense situation. Toss one of these out
every time you see a detour sign. If
you're playing a game like You Can't Say
That, use these detours as the penalty.
(Disclaimer: ALWAYS be safe. If your
mental detour suggests you roll down the
window and scream at a passerby,
be mindful of the neighborhood and
the passerby. Don't put yourself in
harm's way.)

THE FOLLOWING
IS A LIST OF
MENTAL
DETOURS
THAT CAN
LIGHTEN
A TENSE
SITUATION.

DETOURS

- Roll down your window and scream, "Honey, I love you!" to someone standing on the corner.

- Turn to the person next to you and say, "Moogie Moogie Moogie Walla Walla Bing Bang" without giggling.

- Hold your nose, and sing the Barney song.

- Do your best imitation of your mother.

- Do your best imitation of your youth worker.

- Look at a person in another car and slowly put your finger up your nose.

- Do an impression of a farm animal.

- In 60 seconds switch your shoes to the opposite feet. Leave them there for the rest of the day.

- Have the person next to you write down a number between one and ten. Guess the number. If you get it right, stop playing. If you get it wrong, start over. Play until you guess the correct number.

- Choose a friend to help you say, "Peter Piper picked a peck of pickled peppers. A peck of pickled peppers Peter Piper picked." Say this together with each of you saying every other word. See how fast you can go.

- Turn to the nearest person of the opposite sex and say, "Baby, you make my ribs squeak."

- Give the driver a shoulder rub.

- Wiggle something.

- Pick any person (other than the driver) and switch seats.

- Sing a hymn with a Scooby Doo voice.

IN 60 SECONDS SWITCH YOUR SHOES TO THE OPPOSITE FEET. LEAVE THEM THERE FOR THE REST OF THE DAY.

- Roll down the window and scream, "The British are coming!" three times.

- Get a pen and draw a smiley face on someone's big toe.

- Whistle your favorite song, and see who can guess what it is.

- Belch.

- At the next rest stop, see if you can get a stranger's autograph.

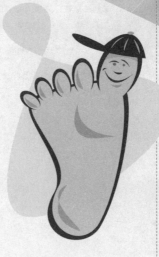

- Try on someone's glasses.

- Tell a story that has a monkey in it.

- Do an impression of an animal.

- Turn upside down.

- At the next rest stop, stand on the sidewalk perfectly still for as long as you can.

- At the next rest stop look up at the sky, and see how many people you can get to look up with you.

- Scratch someone's back.

- At the next rest stop pretend you got your finger hooked in the change compartment of a pay phone.

- At the next rest stop walk around yelling, "Here, Fluffy!" If you are feeling spunky, try yelling, "Mommmmm?"

- Get two or more people in the van to tie their shoelaces together and walk around the rest area together.

AT THE NEXT
REST STOP
PRETEND YOU
GOT YOUR
FINGER
HOOKED IN THE
CHANGE
COMPARTMENT
OF A **PAY**
PHONE.

DETOURS

- Make your hands into a Batman mask and sing, "Batmannnnnnn nanananananananananananana Batmannnnnnnnn!"

- Get three friends to stand with you at the next rest area and pretend you're watching a fireworks show.

- Talk in the third person for the next hour.

- For the next hour, say all of your punctuation out loud.

FOR THE NEXT HOUR, SAY ALL OF YOUR PUNCTUATION OUT LOUD.

fourteen

Let's Talk:
DISCUSSION
QUESTIONS

THESE DISCUSSION QUESTIONS

are designed to pass time when everyone is tired of playing games and
drawing doodles. Discussion questions
work best on long car drives, and they
work best in the evenings when you
can't see what's outside. The questions
are broken down into five categories
with each category based on a common road sign you'll see along the
way. Let the signs to be your guide, or
randomly ask a question from the
book. Categories are:

* Questions about building YOU
* Questions about God and church

DISCUSSION QUESTIONS WORK BEST ON LONG CAR DRIVES, AND THEY WORK BEST IN THE EVENINGS WHEN YOU CAN'T SEE WHAT'S OUTSIDE.

- *Questions about careers*

- *Questions about school*

- *Questions about dating*

Let your students know that "I don't know" and "It depends" are not acceptable answers. However, never force students to answer a question that may make them uncomfortable. Institute a rule that says you can pass on a question but only once. Once the original receiver answers a question, open the question up to the group. Listen to their answers, and come up with questions based on those responses. Encourage them to elaborate. Asking "Why?" is a great way to keep teenagers talking.

Encourage teens to think beyond their limits. A question like, "Where would you go on vacation if you could go anywhere in the world?" may seem limited to kids with little or no money. Tell them to think beyond their boundaries when they answer the questions. It is also important for YOU to remember that most of these are opinion questions. Teenagers explore their faith along with everything else in their lives. They may have an opinion that doesn't necessarily go along with yours or your denomination. Let them explore, and never make them feel as if they are wrong. If they say something that throws up a red flag for you, make a mental note to talk about it later.

HOWEVER, NEVER FORCE STUDENTS TO ANSWER A QUESTION THAT MAY MAKE THEM UNCOMFORTABLE.

Questions about building YOU

- What is your most prized possession? (Family and pets are a given. If the house is burning and the family is safe, what would you go for before you left?)

- If you were going to be on a game show, which one would you choose to be on? Which one do you think you could win and take home the jackpot?

- Could you be best friends with someone who was openly gay? What if it meant people would assume you were, too?

- Which color M&M® is your favorite and why?

- Which kind of M&M® do you prefer? Plain? Peanut? Almond? Mint? Peanut butter? If you could create your own, what would it be?

- What will be the first thing you do the morning after you graduate?

HOW
HAVE YOUR
PARENTS
CHANGED SINCE
YOU WERE
SMALL?

Let's Talk:
DISCUSSION QUESTIONS

WHAT

WAS THE

SCARIEST

THING

THAT EVER

HAPPENED

TO YOU?

- What will you do after you retire?

- If you could take a year off between high school and college and live anywhere in the world, where would you go?

- How have your parents changed since you were small?

- Name the part of the car that is most like you. (Example: I am the battery because I charge people up.)

- If they were going to name a soft drink after you, what would it be called and what would it taste like?

- Name a celebrity who looks most like you.

- What was the best vacation you ever had?

- If you could go back in time for just two minutes, where would you go and what would you do?

- Create a brand new ice cream flavor based on someone else in the car. What would it be called, and what would the flavors be?

- Would you take a pie in the face for $50? What if it were on TV?

- Describe yourself using the name of a candy bar.

- Have you ever tried to find your Christmas gifts before Christmas? What happened?

- Could you run into your school lunchroom wearing just a G-string for $100? How much would it take to get you to do such a thing?

- What was the scariest thing that ever happened to you?

- If you had to take a long car ride and could bring along three fictional characters, who would you bring and why?

- If someone asked Mom and Dad what you did that made them the most proud, what would they say?

- What was the biggest whopper you ever told your parents?

- If you were going to be cremated (after you die, of course), what would you want done with your ashes?

- If someone asked you to be the model for a new PEZ dispenser, would you do it?

- Of the seven dwarves in the Snow White movie, which are you most like?

- If you had $100 to give away all at once to any person or organization, who would get the cash and why?

- If life were a baseball game and you were a player, would you be... a.) pitching, b.) batting c.) in the showers d.) out in left field e.) other

IF SOMEONE **ASKED YOU** TO BE THE **MODEL** FOR A NEW **PEZ DISPENSER,** WOULD YOU **DO IT?**

Let's Talk:
DISCUSSION QUESTIONS

- When it comes right down to it, how important are grades?

- If you didn't have to go to school, would you?

- If you could get a B on every test without studying, but you would NEVER be able to get an A, would you take the deal?

- If you could have a two-minute warning before you died, would you take it?

- What's your all-time favorite cartoon?

- Would you rather go to school with a picture of you or a picture of Jesus on your T-shirt?

- Have you ever skipped a class? What happened?

- Would you rather play with finger paints or blocks?

- Do you choose a breakfast cereal for the taste or the prize?

- What's your favorite movie of all time?

- Who was your hero when you were a kid? Why?

- Who is your hero now? Why?

- The Looney Tunes character that is most like you is...

WHO WAS
YOUR HERO
WHEN YOU
WERE A KID?
WHY?

- Would you ask someone next to you to stop smoking in a restaurant?

- Would you ask a neighbor to take down an offensive sign in his yard?

- Are you more Peter Pan or Jiminy Cricket?

- What would it take to make you believe that God is talking to you?

- Hot dogs: ketchup only or the works?

- If being a Christian required a facial tattoo, would you be one?

- Could you kill someone?

- Do you think Jesus ever got tired of being Jesus?

- Do you like surprises?

- Is there any way pain can be good?

- What is the most important thing you've ever done?

- If you could choose one superpower, what would it be?

- Who is the person you just can't stand? What if you knew you were going to sit next to them at God's table?

- If you found a treasure map that looked authentic and could possibly lead you to a

WHO IS THE PERSON YOU JUST CAN'T STAND? WHAT IF YOU KNEW YOU WERE GOING TO SIT NEXT TO THEM AT GOD'S TABLE?

Let's Talk:
DISCUSSION QUESTIONS

WHAT

TRAIT

DO YOU

ADMIRE

IN OTHER

PEOPLE

THAT YOU

DO NOT

HAVE?

treasure but would take you out of the country, would you find a way to go?

- What is the highest spot you've ever been to? (Plane not allowed)

- If you could morph any one part of your face, would you? Suppose the change were permanent?

- Can you dance like an idiot in front of other people?

- Imagine you can put on a mask and pass as anyone else for one day. Who would you choose to be?

- What is the biggest impact your parents have had on you so far?

- Describe your wedding.

- Describe your funeral.

- If you could become a bird for one day, would you? What if that involved all the risks and requirements of being a bird?

- Can you worship next to someone you can't stand?

- Could you post bail for your brother or sister regardless of their crime?

- In your opinion, what is power?

- What is the rudest thing you've ever done?

- Which monster is most like you?

- Name your favorite food and your favorite food for your soul.

- What trait do you admire in other people that you do not have?

- What meal would they name after you at a greasy-spoon diner? What about at a fancy restaurant?

- Do you prefer the beach or snow?

- Who would you most want to dress like?

- How would you feel if you heard your parent lie to get out of a traffic ticket?

- What would you do if you overheard your parents talking about you?

- Could you lead a demonstration against a political issue you felt was unfair?

- Have you ever tried to quit a bad habit? What happened?

- When is it okay to judge others?

- Imagine you've been on a deserted island for four years. What would you do the first day after your return home?

- At what point do you tell on a friend?

- If you could name a star, what would it be?

WHEN
IS IT
OKAY TO
JUDGE
OTHERS?

Let's Talk:
DISCUSSION
QUESTIONS

HOW DO YOU
RECEIVE
COMPLIMENTS?
HOW DO YOU
RECEIVE
INSULTS?

- If you could name an element in the Periodic Table, what would it be?

- When is it okay to lie to your parents?

- When it is okay for adults to lie to their parents?

- If you could create a playground and not be restricted by money, what would it look like? What if the laws of physics did not restrict it?

- Are there some things that should never be joked about?

- True or False: "You don't get something for nothing."

- Have you ever told someone you were sorry when you weren't?

- Would you rather lose an arm or a leg or an eye?

- Have you ever taken more than one free sample?

- How would you feel if you found out your mother had an abortion before she had you?

- What are you willing to die for?

- What are your addictions?

- How do you receive compliments? How do you receive insults?

- What is a waste of time?

- If you could invent something that made life easier, what would it be?

- What is your most unused emotion?

- If you won a million dollars, how much would you share and with whom?

- Have you ever embarrassed your parents?

- What if you got famous for all the wrong reasons?

- Have you ever walked out of a movie?

- Have you ever got caught seeing a movie you weren't allowed to see?

- If you had a chance to meet a time-warp-future-version of your best friend, would you? Would you meet the 20-year-old version of yourself?

- Is life fair?

- What if you got completely lost in a city? Would you try to find your way back to where you started, or would you get help? Does it matter if you are on foot or driving?

- Have you ever been a lost child?

- Could you enter a beauty contest? (NOT do you think you're pretty enough, but could you actually enter and go through the process?)

WHAT IF YOU GOT FAMOUS FOR ALL THE WRONG REASONS?

Let's Talk:
DISCUSSION
QUESTIONS

WHAT
WOULD
HAPPEN
IF YOU
SUDDENLY
FOUND
YOURSELF
HOMELESS?

- What are you afraid of?

- When did you last have to deal with a bully?

- What if you broke your grandmother's most prized possession?

- What would you do if you found out your personal hero was arrested for selling drugs?

- What was the most valuable (personally or financially) thing you ever lost? Did you get it back? Do you want it back now?

- What would happen if you suddenly found yourself homeless?

- If doing good deeds became illegal, how long would you stay out of jail?

- Could you be a volunteer at a home for the aged?

- Could you live alone?

Questions about GOD & CHURCH

WHAT WAS THE COOLEST WORSHIP EXPERIENCE YOU EVER HAD?

- Of these three—earth, fire, and water—which one best describes your relationship with God, right now?

- Name a food that you think represents God.

- Is God ever in one place more than another?

- If the lead singer of a heavy-metal-punk-satanic-gangsta-rap band put out a CD of worship music (and it was REALLY good worship music), would you use it in your church?

- True or False: The Bible is a rule book that must be followed to the letter.

- Would you rather sing a solo or preach a sermon?

- What was the coolest worship experience you ever had?

- Do you need church to be religious?

- Can you think of the first time God was more than a word to you?

- Could God be female?

- Does God answer all prayers?

- Do you believe in angels?

- Do you have a favorite Bible verse or passage? What is it?

- Is there any religion that you consider wrong?

- Why do people put a plastic Jesus on their dashboard? Do you have a nativity set in your home?

IS THERE

ANYTHING

IN THE

SCRIPTURES

THAT YOU

QUESTION?

- If you had a dream that seemed very, very real in which God told you to become a minister, would you?

- When was the last time you attended a worship service outside of your denomination or religion?

- Do you believe those people who claim to have had near-death experiences?

- Describe God.

- If you were told to color a picture of God but could only use one crayon, what color would you choose?

- Do you believe a fish swallowed Jonah?

- If you could change one thing about your church service, what would it be?

- Is God watching us on this drive right now?

- Is there anything in the Scriptures that you question?

- Who is (or was) your favorite Sunday school teacher?

- What did you think heaven was like when you were a kid?

- Is Hitler in heaven?

- Describe heaven.

- Define the Holy Spirit.

- If your church were going to hang a giant portrait of Jesus in the sanctuary, what would it look like?

- Should hymns be rewritten to have gender-inclusive language? (Example: "Good Christian Friends, Rejoice")

- Can a minister ban someone from the church property?

- Could you worship sitting next to a convicted child molester?

- Do you believe you will have a body in heaven?

WHAT DID YOU THINK HEAVEN WAS LIKE WHEN YOU WERE A KID?

Let's Talk:
DISCUSSION QUESTIONS

- How would your congregation take it if the entire bulletin were printed in reverse order?

- Would you rather worship God in a group of 5,000 or in a group of 5? Why?

- If you could put a Bible verse on the back of your car, what would it be? What if you could print on a candy bar? A roll of breath mints?

- Is it okay to display a picture of Jesus in a Hawaiian shirt and khakis? Is it okay to show a picture of Jesus laughing? Is there any thing that you consider too far out?

- Do you have a guardian angel?

- If your religion required you to wear a uniform, as in the Salvation Army, or a nun's habit, would you rethink your beliefs?

DO YOU
HAVE A
GUARDIAN
ANGEL?

- What was the last big change of thinking you had with your religion?

- Imagine a biblical amusement park. Now think of a ride depicting your favorite Scripture passage or Bible story.

- What if authentic scrolls were found that seemed to be the writing of Jesus when he was 60?

- What if one of the TV networks came up with a series about Jesus' teen years?

- If you had to design the cover of a Bible for teenagers, what would it look like?

- Would you rather be baptized with a drop of water or in a lake?

- Certain denominations believe that a minister can bless someone or something. What does it mean to be blessed? Have you ever been blessed?

- Mission trips: local or far away? Justify your answer.

- If a well-respected authority told you that the disciples prayed by pulling on their big toes, would you change the way you pray? Why do we consider the classic kneeling-and-folded-hands the position for prayer?

- Come up with a brand new ice cream flavor based on your favorite Bible character.

- What is the difference between a full immersion baptism and a drop of water on the head?

- If Jesus were in a band, what would he play?

- If Jesus were in the Olympics, what would be his sport?

- Come up with a movie line Arnold Schwarzenegger might say if he were cast in the role of Moses.

- Is there anyone who should not be allowed to come into your church and worship next to you? Why?

WHAT IF GOD WERE A CHILD?

Let's Talk:
DISCUSSION
QUESTIONS

WHAT IF
AN ANCIENT
TEXT WAS
DISCOVERED
THAT SAID
JESUS HAD
A WIFE
AND KIDS?

- How important is measuring church attendance?

- What if God were a child?

- What if the only way to make God hear your prayers were through animal sacrifice?

- What if heaven looked exactly like it did in the kiddie Sunday school material? (clouds, robes, harps, wings)

- What if you went to heaven and found out you still had to go to work or school?

- If your schoolteacher decided to use the last five minutes of class time to talk about her own religious beliefs, would you complain?

- Why do some people switch churches frequently and others stay in the same place no matter what happens?

- What if the new stained glass window in your church depicted God as a black woman?

- What if an ancient text was discovered that said Jesus had a wife and kids?

- What if your favorite Christian singer decided to get a new image and dressed in provocative outfits and sang songs about sex?

- If your church told you it was morally wrong to ride roller coasters, would you stop riding roller coasters?

- If biblical scholars and archeologists concluded that Jesus never wore a beard, how far do you think the new image would go?

- Imagine that the company that created the "Got Milk" campaign was hired to create a "God Jesus" campaign. What would the ads look like?

- What if a condom company began distributing their product with Scripture verses printed on the wrapper?

- What would Jesus drive?

- Where would Jesus dine?

- Who would Jesus date?

- Make a one-sentence spiritual point using a drive-thru as your illustration.

- Make a one-sentence spiritual point using your favorite sport as your illustration.

- Make a one-sentence spiritual point using your favorite movie as your illustration.

- What if your church choir decided to sing a really beautiful song by Ozzy Osbourne?

- What if your pastor stood up on a Sunday morning and confessed to a multitude of sins and then begged your forgiveness?

- In India, cows are sacred. What are the sacred cows of your faith? What are the sacred cows of your church?

WHAT IF YOUR CHURCH CHOIR DECIDED TO SING A REALLY BEAUTIFUL SONG BY OZZY OSBORNE?

Let's Talk:
**DISCUSSION
QUESTIONS**

IS IT

DIFFICULT

TO LOVE

WITHOUT

CONDITION

AS JESUS

TOLD US

TO DO?

- What if you died and your worst enemy was there at the gates of heaven to greet you?

- Is anger ever healthy? Is it okay to be angry with God?

- What's the difference between going to church and worship? Is there any? Should there be?

- Who is not allowed in heaven?

- What if your minister said something from the pulpit that offended you?

- How easy is it for you to forgive someone?

- What if half of your youth group started going to a bigger and better church down the street?

- How do you explain God to a small child?

- Does any other religion seem attractive to you?

- Is it difficult to love without condition as Jesus told us to do?

- What would you change about your church physically?

- Could you work as a janitor in your own church?

- What counts as a sign from God? How big does it have to be before you believe it?

Questions
about
CAREERS

IF **YOU**
COULD
CHOOSE
ANY
CAREER...
WHAT WOULD
YOU **WANT**
TO BE?

- Would you rather be seen as a hero to your boss and a jerk to your coworkers, or visa versa?

- Could you risk your life as part of your job? Could you be fireman or a cop? Could you be one of those circus performers who perform without a net?

- If you were offered a dream job, but it would only last five years and it meant skipping college, would you take it?

- Could you turn in a fellow employee for stealing? Is there any difference between stealing a hamburger and embezzling thousands of dollars?

- If you could choose any career (forget about education or salary or "I could never do that"), what would you want to be?

- Would you ever consider the military as a career?

- Imagine an amusement park. Somewhere, someplace, somebody had to think all this stuff up. Could you do a job that required you to be at the top of your creative game every day?

- What would you do if your parents did not approve of your career choice?

- Could you work for your mother or father as part of your job? Could you be part of one of those family-run businesses?

- Would you be willing to take a lie detector test as part of a job application process?

- If you could start your own company, what would it be called and what would you do? Would you want to work by yourself or become a corporation?

HOW MUCH
MONEY DO
YOU NEED
(NOT WANT
BUT NEED) TO
BE HAPPY?

- Could you be your mother's boss?

- Could you work for your boyfriend or girl-friend? Could you be his or her boss?

- Would you rather stay at one place until retirement or jump around from job to job?

- How much money do you need (not want but need) to be happy?

- Would you rather be known as the best at your job, or would you want to be a background part of a well-run team?

- Would you rather sit in an office or be on your feet all day outside?

- Could you marry a person who makes three or four times as much as you do?

- Would you rather sit in an office with several people or have a quiet place of your own?

- If you hated your job but loved your coworkers, could you stay at the job?

- If your boss asked you to lie to cover for him, could you do so? Could you lie to cover for yourself? Could you lie to cover the coworker you want to date?

- Imagine that your first job out of college takes you 5,000 miles away, and you can only visit home once every four or five years. Would you take the job?

- Complete this sentence: The person with the easiest job in the world is...

- Complete this sentence: One job I could never do in a million years is...

- If your boss continuously harassed you (male or female), would you quit?

- When you were a little kid, what did you want to be when you grew up?

- Could you do a job that required you dress up as the opposite sex?

- Could you do a job that asked you to do something really gross?

COULD YOU

WORK

ON THE

TOP FLOOR

OF THE

WORLD'S

LARGEST

OFFICE

BUILDING?

Let's Talk:
DISCUSSION QUESTIONS

- How much would you have to earn to be the guy who takes the pie in the face on TV every day?

- Could you work on the top floor of the world's largest office building?

- If you got lucky and hit the lottery and would never ever have to work to earn a living, would you still get a job?

- Could you be a high school teacher?

- Could you do one of those service jobs that require you to be happy and smiling all the time?

- Could you do a job where one mistake could cost someone his or her life?

WHAT JOB
WOULD YOU
LIKE
TO TRY
FOR JUST
ONE DAY?

- Could you work for a company that makes guns, cigarettes, alcohol, or bombs?

- If your boss did something really stupid but only you saw it, would you tell everybody else?

- Could you work for a company where you had to be around your favorite foods all the time? What if it meant you'd get sick of your favorite food and never eat it anymore?

- Think of a job that does not exist or that only one person in the world does. (Example: Nose cleaner on Mount Rushmore)

- Work can be rewarding, but can it be fun?

- Could you work for a company that used questionable manufacturing standards?

- What job would you like to try for just one day?

- What would you think if they lowered the requirement for President of the United States to age 25 instead of 35?

- Could you do a job you loved it if meant you had to stay in one town for the rest of your life?

- Could you travel for a living?

- Is it possible to earn too much money? Should all jobs have a salary cap?

- Could you do a job that required physically hurting someone?

- Could you do a job where every day you risked your life?

- If you could work for the circus, what job would you choose?

- Would you prefer a job that challenged you mentally or physically?

- What if you didn't have to work...ever?

- Which is more important: family or money? What if you had family but lived in a homeless shelter?

IS THERE A JOB UNIFORM THAT YOU WOULD REFUSE TO WEAR?

Let's Talk:
DISCUSSION QUESTIONS

CREATE A
BUMPER
STICKER
SLOGAN
THAT SUMS
UP YOUR
PHILOSOPHY
ABOUT WORK.

- What if you had a really strong opinion on a subject and everyone else at the table thought the opposite?

- What if they were all adults?

- True or False: If you say you'll do it, you'll do it.

- Could you dance for joy? What if you were in the middle of a crowded street?

- Is there a job uniform that you would refuse to wear?

- If you knew your boss was skimming profits, would you report him? What if it meant you'd probably lose your job too?

- Does everybody fudge his or her resume?

- Would you hire a person who's been fired from every other job they had?

- Could you be a minister? Could you be a youth minister?

- Could you be a police officer or firefighter?

- Could you be the person who pulls the switch on the electric chair?

- Would you rather work outside or inside?

- Create a bumper sticker slogan that sums up your philosophy about work.

- Is there such a thing as a harmless lie?

- If your boss told you to take off the cross necklace or be fired, what would you do?

- If you could travel overseas for a job but wouldn't be able to come home for five years, would you go?

- Could you plan funerals for a living? Could you plan your own?

- What if your job was to make the phone calls nobody else wanted to make? (You're fired. Your mother died.)

- Could you administer drivers' tests to 16-year-olds for a living?

- Do you need to be told when you do a good job, or can you continue to work without it?

- Could you fire someone who came to work with a bad attitude? What if it was your best friend?

- How do you explain work to a small child?

- Could you do public speaking as a career?

- Who is your greatest influence, career-wise?

DO YOU **NEED** TO BE **TOLD** WHEN YOU DO A **GOOD JOB,** OR CAN YOU **CONTINUE TO WORK** WITHOUT IT?

Let's Talk:
DISCUSSION
QUESTIONS

Questions about SCHOOL

IF YOUR
TEACHER
ASSIGNED AN
ESSAY
TOPIC
THAT YOU
DID NOT
AGREE WITH,
WHAT WOULD
YOU DO?

- If you could spend a day working in the school cafeteria instead of going to class, would you?

- Could you cross a picket line if your teachers were on strike? Could you support a strike if it jeopardized your graduation?

- Who is or was your absolute favorite teacher? Why?

- What was the best thing you ever said in class?

- If your teacher assigned an essay topic that you did not agree with, what would you do?

- If you could change the current grading system, would you? How?

- Should teachers be tested annually for competency?

- If you could be a teacher in your own school for just one day, would you?

- Whose picture is in your locker? Is yours in someone else's? Do you wish it were?

- What was the dumbest thing you ever said in class?

- Have you ever lied to a teacher? (Example: My dog ate my homework; I wasn't smoking.)

- What kind of test is the hardest to take? (True/false, multiple choice, essay)

- Should schools provide day-care for children of teen mothers?

- Should schools provide free condoms or other birth control?

- Should schools teach sex education?

- Would you ever want to be on the school board?

- Are most of your friends at school in the same grade as you?

- What is your favorite class this year? Of all time?

- How do you intend to get into college? Where do you want to go?

- Will you attend your 20-year high school reunion?

WHAT IS YOUR FAVORITE CLASS THIS YEAR? OF ALL TIME?

WHAT IS THE MOST CONTROVERSIAL THING YOU EVER DISCUSSED IN YOUR SCHOOL?

- Talk about the worst or best school picture you've ever taken.

- Have you ever been in class with someone who reminded the teacher to give homework?

- If the teacher passed out a darken-the-dot test and yours seemed to have all the answers filled in correctly, would you give it back or put your name on it and say nothing? What if it was a college entrance exam?

- Should athletes get special consideration in school? Should anyone?

- If you could get rid of any one class in your schedule, what would it be?

- What if they started offering home economics to only girls and shop to only boys?

- What if they suddenly got rid of grade levels, and you simply graduated when you completed the work?

- Should your school teach a class in social interaction? How about one in etiquette?

- What would you do if your school hung the Ten Commandments in the lunchroom?

- Should a principal be able to chain doors to keep kids in school and drug dealers out?

- What is the most controversial thing you ever discussed in your school?

- How do you think the physical school building has changed since your parents were in school? How do you think it will change by the time your kids are in school?

- What would it take to get kicked off a high school sports team?

- Should teachers teach morals and values?

- At what age should drug education begin?

- Who was the most effective (but not necessarily the favorite) teacher you ever had?

- What if you saw a gun in a friend's locker?

- What if you saw a gun in your teacher's desk?

- What if the teacher nobody liked asked your personal opinion on his or her teaching style?

- Have you ever made straight As on a report card?

- What if your teacher asked your parents to come in for a talk? How would you tell your parents?

- If your teacher accused someone of cheating that you knew was innocent, would you speak up? Would it matter who got caught? Should it?

WHAT IF YOUR **TEACHER ASKED** YOUR **PARENTS** TO **COME IN** FOR **A TALK?**

Let's Talk:
DISCUSSION
QUESTIONS

WOULD YOU

RATHER GO

ON A FIRST

DATE ALONE

OR WITH

ANOTHER

COUPLE?

- Could you go on a second date with someone you didn't have a good time with on the first date?

- The biggest misconception that guys have about girls is....

- The biggest misconception that girls have about guys is...

- When, if ever, do you see marriage in your future?

- If you had a great time on a date and it ended with a peck on the cheek, would you tell your friends it was more the next day?

- Have you ever gone Dutch on a date? Is it unreasonable to expect someone to pay for half the date?

- Would you rather go on a first date alone or with another couple?

- Could you continue to date someone who ordered dinner from a children's menu?

- Talk about a blind date that you had.

- Describe the perfect date.

- If you were on a date and your date got sick and threw up in your car, would you go out with that person again?

- Could you fall in love with someone who was not in your religion? Could you fall in love with an atheist?

- What are the three most important characteristics to look for while on a date?

- Could you fall in love with someone of a different race?

- What are the three (and only three) ways to get AIDS?

- What would you do if a teacher asked you out on a date?

- If you thought your best friend was dating a jerk, would you say something? What if your friend were dating someone really nice who also happened to use or sell drugs?

- A night on the town with dinner and a movie entitles the guy to what at the end of the evening?

- How has dating changed since your parents were going out?

IF YOU **THOUGHT** YOUR BEST **FRIEND** WAS DATING A JERK, WOULD YOU **SAY** SOMETHING?

Let's Talk:
DISCUSSION QUESTIONS

WHAT'S

THE

DIFFERENCE

BETWEEN

DATING

AND

COURTING?

- Can you fall in love with someone you've never met?

- If your best friend's ex asked you out, would you go?

- Tell a date horror story.

- Have you ever gone out with someone because you really wanted to see that movie or go to that party?

- What is the best age to begin car dating?

- What's a reasonable time to be home from a date if you are 16? 17? 14?

- What if your date sent their dinner back to the chef three times? What if you were at a greasy spoon?

- Describe a gentleman.

- Describe a lady.

- How much prep time goes into a date?

- What if the person you most wanted to go out with invited you to go cow tipping or shoplifting on a date?

- If you had a blank-check date, where would you go and what would you do?

- What's the difference between dating and courting?

- Would you rather date or court?

- Would you rather go to a movie or a football game on a date?

- Would you rather be set up by your mother or by your best friend? (Think about this one before you answer.)

- Would you rather go to "Chez Expensive" or "Burger Barn" on a first date?

- Has your parent ever turned out to be right about someone you dated?

- What if all the CDs in your date's boom box were Pat Boone CDs?

- What if your date's parents followed you? What if you didn't find out until the next day?

- What would you do if you went to a movie on a first date and it had a graphic, gratuitous sex scene?

- Would you say, "I had a great time" even if you didn't?

- Is it easier to go out with someone you've known for years?

- Give an example of a great pick-up line. Give an example of a lousy one.

HAS YOUR **PARENT** EVER TURNED OUT TO BE **RIGHT** ABOUT **SOMEONE** YOU **DATED?**

Let's Talk:
DISCUSSION
QUESTIONS

WHEN
IS IT "TOO
SOON" TO
FALL IN
LOVE?
DO YOU NEED
TO BE A
CERTAIN
AGE?

- What if your date asked you to go steady at the end of the first date?

- Finish this sentence: Dating is like a balloon because...

- Finish this sentence: Dating is like a refrigerator because...

- If your boyfriend or girlfriend failed a grade, would you still go out with them?

- When is "too soon" to fall in love? Do you need to be a certain age?

- Have you ever seen your parents be romantic?

- What if you knew your date was lying to you about his or her past?

- What if you found out your date shared a secret you told her?

- If the food came to the table late and cold, would you send it back? Would you complain to the manager?

- If you were invited on a date you knew would be boring, would you still go?